BUILDING THE NEW AMERICAN ECONOMY

JEFFREY D. SACHS

Foreword by
BERNIE SANDERS

BUILDING THE NEW AMERICAN ECONOMY

SMART, FAIR, AND SUSTAINABLE

Columbia University Press
New York

Columbia University Press

Publishers Since 1893

New York   Chichester, West Sussex

cup.columbia.edu

Copyright © 2017 Jeffrey D. Sachs

Cataloging-in-Publication Data available
from the Library of Congress

ISBN 978-0-231-18404-5 (cloth)
ISBN 978-0-231-54528-0 (electronic)

Columbia University Press books are printed
on permanent and durable acid-free paper.

Printed in the United States of America

Cover design: Lisa Hamm

For Sienna, Willa, and Olive
and their generation

CONTENTS

CONTENTS

FOREWORD

BERNIE SANDERS

United States Senator from Vermont

My campaign for President of the United States was never just about electing a president. It was about transforming America. As I traveled all across this great country of ours, I had the honor of meeting countless Americans who desperately want an economy that works for the middle class and working families, not just the billionaire class. They are sick and tired of working longer hours for lower wages, while multinational corporations ship millions of jobs overseas. They are fed up with an economy in which CEOs make 300 times more than they do, while 52 percent of all new income goes to the top one percent. They are tired of not being able to afford decent, quality childcare or a college education for their kids. They want policies that create jobs, raise wages, and protect the most vulnerable people in this country. And they want us to aggressively combat climate change to make our planet healthy and habitable for future generations.

What I heard and what I continue to hear is that Americans have had enough of establishment politicians and establishment economists who have claimed for far too long that we must choose between economic growth, economic fairness, and environmental sustainability. They have sold us a bill of goods that says we can't have all three. Well, they are wrong. To my mind, widely shared prosperity, economic fairness, and environmental sustainability must go hand in hand. An economy in which almost all of the wealth and income flows to the very top is simply not sustainable. Likewise, an economy based on destructive environmental policies will inevitably lead to catastrophe for rich and poor alike.

In this book, Columbia University Professor Jeffrey Sachs presents a clear explanation of how America can achieve all three critically important goals and create an economy that works for all of us. Jeffrey Sachs is one of the world's leaders in the field of sustainable development, which takes a serious look at the economic, social, and environmental impacts of development policies. I am proud to say that he was also a strong supporter and close advisor to me during the presidential campaign and a key ally of our progressive revolution to transform America.

This book is particularly timely given the election of Donald Trump. The president-elect tapped into the anger of the declining middle class, but he left unchallenged much of the economic orthodoxy that led to the hemorrhaging of middle-class jobs in the first place. He promised economic prosperity, in large part, by providing trillions of dollars in tax breaks to the wealthy and large corporations, and by turning back efforts to curb the carbon emissions from fossil fuel that contribute to climate change. And instead of offering a plan to insure the 28 million Americans who still don't have health-care coverage, he pledged to repeal President Obama's Affordable Care Act. That would throw 20 million Americans off of health insurance.

Professor Sachs offers a very different vision for America on a wide range of issues, including the federal budget, infrastructure, jobs, health care, climate change, and foreign policy. He explains where America can and should be by 2030, in terms of reducing poverty, addressing the scourge of suffocating student debt, expanding health care and lowering costs, protecting the environment, and many other issues. Now, more than ever, this is a message that needs to be heard.

PREFACE

Donald Trump becomes president of a nation that is deeply divided by class, race, health, and opportunity. In his acceptance speech, he pledged to be the president for all Americans. He also gave a very promising hint of how to pursue that objective in practice.

Trump is a real-estate developer, so it's not surprising that his brief acceptance speech was dominated by the idea of "rebuilding," a word he mentioned four times:

> Working together, we will begin the urgent task of rebuilding our nation and renewing the American dream. . . . We are going to fix our inner cities and rebuild our highways, bridges, tunnels, airports, schools, hospitals. We're going to rebuild our infrastructure, which will become, by the way, second to none. And we will put millions of our people to work as we rebuild it.

This is a valid, indeed uplifting perspective. America desperately needs rebuilding. Its infrastructure is decrepit; its energy system is out of date for a climate-threatened economy; its coastal areas are already showing grave vulnerability to rising sea levels and extreme storms; its Rust Belt cities like Grand Rapids, Michigan, are boarded up; its inner cities across the country are unhealthy for the children being raised in them. Rebuilding America's inner cities and creating a twenty-first-century infrastructure could be Trump's greatest legacy.

Trump's pledge to make America's infrastructure "second to none" is a correct and bold goal, for America's competitiveness, future job creation, public health, and wellbeing. Yet as I will explain in this book, America today is certainly no longer "second to none." On a recent Sustainable Development Goals Index, the United States ranked twenty-second out of thirty-four high-income countries. For Americans returning from foreign travel, the well-known sign that they've touched down at home is that the elevators, escalators, and moving walkways of our once-proud airports are out of order.

A builder-president could indeed help to restore vitality to the U.S. economy and put millions to work in the process. All of the major candidates in the 2016 campaign pledged a major effort to build America's infrastructure. Indeed, Trump suggested a hefty price tag of $1 trillion, which is a realistic sum and target for the coming five years (roughly 1 percent of national income per year).

The keys to success in building the new America economy can be summarized in three words: smart, fair, and sustainable.

A smart economy means deploying the best of cutting-edge technology. Our energy grids should be smart in economizing on energy use and in incorporating distributed energy sources (such as wind and solar power) into the grid. Our transport system should be smart in enabling self-driving electric vehicles within our cities and twenty-first-century high-speed rail between them.

A fair economy would start with Trump's pledge to rebuild the inner cities. Such a pledge should include affordable housing; decent urban public schools and public health facilities; efficient transport services for low-income communities; parks and green spaces in places now burdened by urban blight; the cleanup of urban toxic dumps; comprehensive recycling rather than landfills; and safe water for all Americans, so that the drinking-water disaster that afflicts Flint, Michigan, and similar crises elsewhere are brought to a rapid end and never recur.

A sustainable economy means acknowledging and anticipating the dire environmental threats facing America's cities and infrastructure. The vulnerability of New Orleans levees had been predicted by scientists and engineers long before Hurricane Katrina. The flooding of New York City had been predicted long before Hurricane Sandy. The risks ahead to the United States in the event of unchecked climate change can be found in countless scientific and policy studies, such as Risky Business and the National Climate Assessment.[1]

Much could go wrong in an undirected building boom that is not smart, fair, and sustainable. Trump's campaign pledges to restore the Keystone XL Pipeline and U.S. coal production are cases in point. Investing in a boom in fossil fuels would be an expensive dead end. Such projects will inevitably be closed soon after they are completed, if not in a Trump administration then in the ones that follow. They are simply untenable environmentally, no matter what the lobbyists assert. Billions of dollars would be thrown down the drain to develop resources that will never be used.

It's funny that climate deniers are chortling about the incoming Trump administration. Nature doesn't care what they think, and neither do the 192 other countries on the planet that signed the recent Paris Climate Agreement. Fossil fuel companies can spend money developing unusable resources, but they would be throwing money down the mineshaft, as would the investors buying the bonds financing such hapless projects.

Trump made another very important pledge in his acceptance speech that should underpin a successful strategy for building the new American economy:

> I will harness the creative talents of our people, and we will call upon the best and brightest to leverage their tremendous talent for the benefit of all.

America has nearly 5,000 colleges and universities across the country, including every congressional district, with the finest collection of engineering and scientific faculty and knowledge in the world. These institutions of higher learning have schools of public policy, social work, public health, business administration, and environmental science. Most importantly, they have 21 million young Americans enrolled to gain expertise in the skills needed for leadership and skills in the twenty-first century.

By harnessing the vast brainpower and experience in our colleges and universities, in civil society and business, America could indeed enter an era of successful rebuilding, one that creates a smart, fair, and sustainable economy that is truly second to none, and that serves as an inspiration for other parts of the world.

This book offers an up-to-date look at America's opportunities and challenges as the new Trump administration and Congress take office. I recommend that the United States adopt the Sustainable Development Goals, suitably adapted to its specific conditions and needs, as key guideposts for building the new economy. It is our task, across the nation, to build a new economy that is smart, fair, and sustainable.

I hope that the evidence and ideas in this book will help to meet this enormous and shared task of our era.

Jeffrey D. Sachs
November 10, 2016
New York City

ACKNOWLEDGMENTS

This book emerged from a series of op-eds in the *Boston Globe* in the fall of 2016. I want to thank the *Globe*'s wonderful and celebrated op-ed page editor Marjorie Pritchard for her ideas, enthusiasm, and inimitable editorial support and guidance in preparing these pieces. The *Boston Globe* is a glorious paper that I still consider to be my "hometown" paper following my thirty years living in the Boston area from 1972 to 2002.

My enormous gratitude also goes to my academic hometown press, the Columbia University Press. There is a great joy for a university professor to work with one's own university press, but the joy is greatly magnified when the press is a justly world-renowned scholarly publisher. I am thrilled that Columbia University Press published my previous book (*The Age of Sustainable Development*, 2015) and also enthusiastically supported this project. My special thanks go to Bridget Flannery-McCoy for her energy and help at every stage and for expediting the publication schedule so that this book came out in time for the incoming Trump administration and Congress in January 2017. Also, I am grateful to Patrick Fitzgerald, editor for the life sciences and sustainability, for his continuing confidence and support.

ACKNOWLEDGMENTS

My special assistant, Ms. Mariam Gulaid, helped me at every stage to produce this book, as always with her great accuracy and unbounded good cheer.

And of course my thanks are endlessly due to my wife, Sonia, my partner in everything, and my wonderfully wise and inspiring children, Lisa, Adam, and Hannah, who work very hard trying to keep their father on track.

BUILDING THE
NEW AMERICAN
ECONOMY

1

WHY WE NEED TO BUILD A NEW AMERICAN ECONOMY

My purpose in this book is to explore the economic choices facing the United States and its relations with the rest of the world at the start of the new administration of President Donald Trump and the new Congress. One reason why Washington has been in gridlock for years is that both parties have pursued a deeply flawed vision for America. The Republicans have called for a smaller government when we need a government that does more and better to address slow economic growth, rising inequality, and dire environmental threats. Democrats have called for a larger government but without clear thinking about priorities, programs, management, and finances for an expanded role.

This book charts a better course for American public policy based on long-term societal objectives around the concept of sustainable development. I outline a strategy of scaled-up investments, both public and private, and the means to finance them. I emphasize throughout that the way to break Washington's gridlock is to build a new national consensus based on local brainstorming in every part of the country. President Trump and the Congress will remain stymied until they both hear from people across the United States that the time for major change has arrived, with clear goals, policy direction, and financing.

My core contention is that with the right choices, America's economic future is bright. Indeed, we are the lucky beneficiaries of a revolution in technologies that can raise prosperity, slash poverty, increase leisure time, extend healthy lives, and protect the environment. It sounds good, perhaps too good to be true; but it is true. The pervasive pessimism—that American children today will grow up to worse living standards than their parents—is a real possibility, but not an inevitability.

The most important concept about our economic future is that it is our choice and in our hands, both individually and collectively as citizens.

The reasons for the pessimism are real. The United States is experiencing the lowest growth rates in the postwar era. Economic growth recorded since the 2008 financial crisis has been about half of what was forecast in mid-2009: 1.4 percent annual growth from 2009 to 2015 compared with a projected growth rate of 2.7 percent. Around 81 percent of American households, according to a recent McKinsey study, experienced flat or falling incomes between 2005 and 2014[1]. At the same time, the inequality of income has soared over the past 35 years, adding to the concentration of wealth and income among the top 1 percent of the population. In 1980, the top 1 percent took home 10 percent of household income; in 2015, it was around 22 percent.[2]

While unemployment has declined, from a peak of 10 percent in October 2009 in the depths of the recent financial crisis to the current low rate of around 5.0 percent, part of that recovery has been achieved because individuals of working age have left the labor force entirely, out of frustration at low-paying jobs or no job opportunities at all. The ratio of overall employment relative to the working age (25–54) population has declined from 81.5 percent in 2000 to 77.2 percent in 2015.

If this were not enough, the headwinds seem set to continue. The antitrade sentiments from both political parties over the 2016 election season, leading both Donald Trump and Hillary Clinton to reject a draft trade agreement with Asia, reflects a widespread feeling that America has lost jobs in large numbers to low-wage competition with China and other countries, and that more such job losses are to come. Recent research suggests that such fears, long scoffed at by economists, are based on reality.[3] U.S. manufacturing sector jobs have shifted overseas, as well as being lost to automation. U.S. counties on the front lines of competition with Chinese manufacturing have experienced the largest job losses.

Automation has become another source of high anxiety. Here, too, economists have generally scoffed at the public fears that machines will take away our jobs.[4] Hasn't the entire industrial era proved that view wrong? they ask rhetorically. Haven't new machines and technology always created more jobs than they have cost? These questions are fair, but so too are the worries. The advent of smart machines seems to be shifting income from workers to capital, driving down wages, and contributing to the frustration low-wage workers feel about finding a job with a livable wage. Some workers do seem to be squeezed right out of the labor force, and the share of labor earnings in national income is falling, a sign that decent jobs indeed are being overtaken by the robots.

So, yes, Americans have the right to lots of economic fears: of Wall Street traders who destabilize the economy; of the top 1 percent who corral the lion's share of economic growth; and of jobs and wages lost to China and the robots. But there are still more reasons to worry.

The federal budget deficit in 2016 was around 2.9 percent of gross domestic product (GDP,) but given current trends will rise to around 4 percent of GDP in the coming years. The consequence of chronically high budget deficits is rapidly increasing public debt. The Treasury debt owed to the public here and abroad has soared from 35 percent of U.S. GDP at the end of 2007 to 75 percent at the end of 2015. The Congressional Budget Office warns that under current fiscal policies, the debt is likely to reach around 86 percent of GDP by 2026 and 110 percent of GDP by 2036.[5]

Debt sustainability is one part of the future we leave to today's children. Environmental sustainability is, of course, the other. And if there is one endangered elephant in the room, one existential worry to keep us up at night, it is the relentless, punishing, ongoing damage that Americans and the rest of the world are doing to the environment. We can't rest easy on our economic future, and I would not advise doing so for a moment, until we find a path to climate safety and true sustainability for our water, air, and biodiversity. Most importantly, we need to overhaul the energy system, to shift our reliance from carbon-based energy—coal, oil, and gas— to noncarbon energy sources—wind, solar, hydro, nuclear, and others that do not cause global warming. Fortunately, America is replete with renewable energy resources. But there are many other steps we need to take to achieve environmental sustainability, and I'll get into those in more detail in the chapters to come.

Finally, add to these challenges our nation's highly divisive and corrupted politics, and it's not hard to be gloomy. Some leading economists have even declared the end of two centuries of economic growth. We are, to use their jargon, in a new era of "secular stagnation." And if growth is at an end, social stability could be jeopardized as well, with the economy turning into a zero-sum struggle wherein the gains for some groups must be the losses for others.

The doyen of the pessimists (and author of a wonderful new book, *The Rise and Fall of American Growth*), Robert Gordon, says we've simply run out of big new inventions to keep the economic engine going.[6] Gordon argues that smartphones and the Internet simply don't measure up to mega-breakthroughs like the steam engine, electricity, TV and radio, the automobile, and aviation—the great technological drivers of two centuries of economic advance.

My argument, to be detailed over the course of this book, is that the pessimists have a point—indeed, several of them—but that overall they are mistaken. We are not at the end of progress, at least not if we get our act together. And we can. Even the political paralysis can end if we can discern more accurately and clearly the right path out of our very real and complicated problems. America has confronted and overcome many horrendously large problems in the past—the Great Depression, Nazism and Stalinism, the political exclusion of African Americans, the poverty and heavy disease burden of the elderly—and can do so again.

My starting point is a concept, sustainable development, which conveys a new and better approach to national problem solving. Luckily, it's a concept that's been around for a while, long enough that we have an extensive body of knowledge and extensive evidence of what to do. And long enough to be acknowledged widely not only by scientists, engineers, and a growing number of investors but also by governments around the world. On September 25, 2015, all 193 governments of

FIGURE 1.1 The Seventeen Sustainable Development Goals

the United Nations adopted sustainable development, with seventeen specific Sustainable Development Goals (SDGs), as the basis for global cooperation on economic and social development during the coming fifteen years (see figure 1.1).[7] On December 12, 2015, the same governments adopted the Paris climate agreement, also built on the concept of sustainable development.[8]

Sustainable development argues that economic policy works best when it focuses simultaneously on three big issues: first, promoting economic growth and decent jobs; second, promoting social fairness to women, the poor, and minority groups; and third, promoting environmental sustainability. American economic policy has tended in recent years to focus only on the first, economic growth, and not done that very well, in part because it has largely neglected the growing crises of economic inequality and environmental ruin, even as those have worsened dramatically in recent years. Now, because of our multiple policy failures and unbalanced growth, even future economic growth itself is imperiled.

Economic growth, social fairness, and environmental sustainability are mutually supportive, and future growth now depends on addressing the two neglected pillars of sustainable development. *Choosing* our economic future is the key idea. Economies don't just grow, achieve fairness, and protect the environment of their own accord. Economic theory and experience make clear that there is no "invisible hand" that produces economic growth, much less sustainable development. Even Adam Smith was clear on that point, and wrote Book V of *The Wealth of Nations* to emphasize the role of government in infrastructure and education.

But how do we choose? Mainly, we choose our economic future through the decisions we make concerning saving and investment. Societies, like individuals, face the challenge of "delayed gratification": We achieve future growth by holding back on current consumption and by investing instead in future knowledge, technology, education, skills, health, infrastructure, and environmental protection. And if we invest well, we hit the trifecta, achieving an economy that is smart, fair, and sustainable. Such an economy will create decent jobs, ensure ample leisure, promote public health, and underpin competitiveness in a highly competitive world economy.

Investing well, in turn, will require two things on which America is decidedly out of practice, so much so that even the hint of them will cause many to squirm. The first is planning. We need to plan for our future. I can recall when the very idea of planning became a dirty word, associated with the "central planning" of the defunct Soviet Union. Yet we need planning now more than ever to overcome complex challenges such as overhauling our energy system, an effort that will require decades of concerted action.

The second is the need for more public investment to spur private investment. Ever since Ronald Reagan told us "Government is not the solution to our problem; government is the problem," we have cut public investment to the bone. We experience it every day with decrepit highways, bridges, levees, and urban water systems; aging airports and seaports; and neglected hazardous waste sites. Yet without government's role in building infrastructure and guiding the energy transition, private investors—with trillions of dollars under management—will remain stuck on the sidelines, not knowing where to place their bets.

With breakthroughs in smarter machines and information systems, new materials, remote sensing, advanced biotechnology, and much more, there are innumerable ways forward toward sustainable development and higher living standards, including healthier lives and more leisure. But can a complex modern society actually achieve these goals and balance the budget at the same time? I'm going to show why the answer is yes and, even better, look to other countries that are ahead of the United States and are forging the way to the future in meeting certain key challenges such as education, skills training, fairness, and low-carbon energy.

In a recent study, my colleagues and I measured how 149 countries, including the United States, stack up on sustainable development and, notably, on the progress that the countries will need to make to achieve the recently adopted SDGs. The news was eye opening, sobering, but also strangely inspiring. The United States came in twenty-second out of thirty-four high-income countries, far from the lead held by Sweden,

FIGURE 1.2 Ranking of the SDGs Among the OECD Countries (on 0 to 100 scale, with 100 as the best possible score)

Denmark, Norway, and Switzerland, respectively (figure 1.2). Canada came in eleventh. Coming in twenty-second may seem a bit depressing for a country that likes to think of itself as first, but it's also exciting to know that we can learn from others as we seek our own way forward.[9]

In the chapters that follow, I will go into depth on these key points: the future budget choices, including tax reform; moving toward safe, renewable energy (SDGs 7 and 13); fighting inequality (SDG 10); creating good jobs alongside the robots (SDG 8); making trade deals work for all (SDG 17); slashing our outlandish health care costs (SDG 3); and achieving a long-delayed peace dividend (SDG 16). We shall see that we do indeed have choices, good ones, that can deliver renewed progress and sustainable development for America.

2

INVESTMENT, SAVING, AND
U.S. LONG-TERM GROWTH

Long-term economic growth in the United States has been
slowing for decades. Robert Gordon, I noted in chapter 1,
has argued that the period of rapid U.S. growth, from
1920 to 1970, was a golden age never to be revisited. Several
economists have joined Gordon in arguing that we have
entered an age of secular stagnation. This kind of fatalism
is misplaced. The United States, and the world, can achieve
rapid economic progress in the coming decades, but only if we
address the root causes of slower growth.

First, let's do some statistical housekeeping. One year's
GDP growth doesn't tell us too much. GDP data are regularly
revised, so that a few quarters of slow growth could be a mere
aberration of the data. Even if it's real, one slow year might
signify little when growth is averaged over several years. And
GDP growth itself is a deeply flawed measure of wellbeing.
High growth does not guarantee shared economic improvement, and slow growth does not necessarily imply widespread
economic hardship. In recent decades, most of the fruits of
U.S. growth have gone to the richest of the rich, who least
need them.

Still, even after accounting for data errors, short-term cycles, and the yawning gaps between GDP and wellbeing, there is little doubt that the U.S. economy is failing to raise living standards at the same pace as in the past. Annual growth of GDP averaged 3.4 percent per year between 1980 and 2000, but only half of that, 1.7 percent per year, between 2000 and 2014. Since the United States is a high-income country, slow growth is not necessarily a catastrophe (compared, say, with extreme poverty, war, or environmental degradation), yet the U.S. economy has room for major improvement.

The big mistake of "secular stagnationists" is to treat the slowdown of U.S. growth as inevitable, a consequence of the drying up of technological opportunities for future economic improvement. Such fatalism is misguided. Long-term economic improvement occurs when societies invest adequately in their future. The harsh fact is that the United States has stopped investing adequately in the future; slow U.S. economic growth is the predictable and regrettable result.

Although simple measures of national saving are flawed, they convey useful information. The evidence suggests that the U.S. national saving rate has declined markedly since the "Golden Age" celebrated by Gordon. The saving rate is measured in two ways: as "gross saving" before subtracting capital depreciation, or as "net saving" after subtracting depreciation, both relative to national income. The net saving rate has declined more than the gross saving rate because capital depreciation as a share of national income has risen in recent decades (see figure 2.1).

We should also examine separately the net saving rates of the private economy (business and households) and government. We find that both private and government saving rates have declined by roughly the same amount, each by roughly

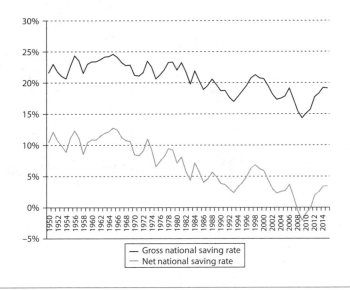

FIGURE 2.1 Gross and Net National Saving Rate (percent of GDP)

5 percentage points of national income. Households are not saving as much of their income as they did decades ago. Government (combining federal, state, and local levels) has gone from a net saving rate near zero to a chronic negative net saving rate (see figure 2.2).

There are several possible causes. Depreciation of capital is certainly absorbing more of gross saving, as we would expect in a capital-rich, mature economy. Households are aging. And government has turned populist, promising tax cuts at every election cycle, thereby denying the government the revenues needed to provide public services, social insurance, and public investments in America's future.

The share of domestic investment in GDP has declined alongside the decline in national saving, though by slightly less as America has borrowed from the rest of the world to

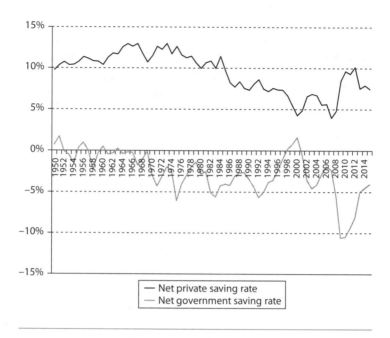

FIGURE 2.2 Government and Private Net Saving Rate
(percent of GDP)

offset part of the decline in saving. Figure 2.3 shows both the gross investment rate and the net investment rate, both as a share of GDP, where net investment equals gross investment minus depreciation. Gross investment as a share of GDP has declined by around 3 percentage points since the 1960s. Net investment has declined by even more, around 5 percentage points, as depreciation relative to GDP has increased. The clear message is that both net saving and investment have declined markedly as a share of GDP, contributing significantly to the decline in long-term growth.

With higher saving and investment rates, both public and private, directed towards productive capital, the United States

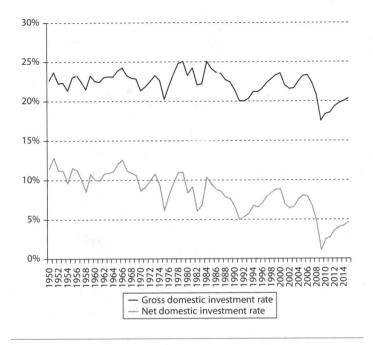

FIGURE 2.3 Gross and Net Domestic Investment (as a share of GDP)

could overcome secular stagnation. The benefits of new scientific and technological breakthroughs—in genomics, nanotechnology, computation, robotics, renewable energy, and more—are certainly within grasp, but only if we invest in their development and uptake. It is especially shocking that at a time when we need new clean energy sources, more nutritious foods, better educational strategies, and smarter cities, we have been cutting the share of national income that government devotes to investments in basic and applied sciences.

In the 1960s, around 4 percent of the federal budget was spent on nondefense research and development (R&D). Now only around 1.5 percent of the budget goes for civilian R&D.

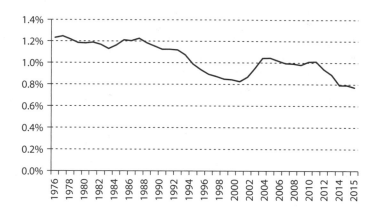

FIGURE 2.4 Federal Civilian R&D as a Share of National Income, 1976–2015

As a share of GDP, total federal R&D declined from around 1.23 percent in 1967 to just 0.77 percent in 2015 (see figure 2.4). In the pursuit of tax cuts, we have undermined our collective ability to build a more prosperous and sustainable future. And we've done it with little recognition of the long-term consequences.

We certainly notice the crumbling of the roads, bridges, and dams that suffer from chronic undersaving and underinvestment. We are less aware of the science, skills, and natural capital that we are shortchanging as well. And we are less aware still that investing in our future requires robust rates of public and private saving. Golden ages don't just happen; they reflect societies that choose to save and invest vigorously in their long-term wellbeing.

To restore growth, therefore, we need to restore investment spending. And to restore investment spending, we will need three things. First, the government should raise tax revenues to fund greater public investments. Yes, it is true that some public investments can and should be debt financed, but in view of the prospects of rising budget deficits in future years, described in the next chapter, it will also be necessary to raise government revenues to pay for part of the new public investments.

Second, the government will need to restore its capacity to plan complex public investments. In recent years, nearly every major infrastructure project has become tied up in regulatory knots and public controversy. Often there is no long-term strategy, but only short-term deal making that drains the confidence of the public. In the days of the national highway program (from the mid-1950s to mid-1970s) and the moonshot (during the 1960s), the public had the sense that the federal government had a plan and a strategy to achieve it.

Third, and perhaps most crucially, we need financial system reform, to shift Wall Street from high-frequency trading and hedge fund insider trading back to long-term capital formation. We remember J. P. Morgan as a titan of finance not for shaving a nanosecond from high-frequency stock market trades, but because his banking firm financed much of America's new industrial economy of the early twentieth century, including steel, railroads, industrial machinery, consumer appliances, and the newly emergent telephone system. U.S. Steel, AT&T, General Electric, International Harvester, and much of the rail industry all bear his financial imprint. If Wall Street continues as a hodgepodge of insider trading, hedge funds, and other wealth management, it will be overtaken by index funds requiring little more than a computer program to operate.

Wall Street's true future vocation should be to underwrite the new age of sustainable investments in renewable energy, smart grids, self-driving electric vehicles, the Internet of Things (connecting smart machines in integrated urban systems), high-speed rail, broadband-connected schools and hospitals, and other strategic investments of the new era. Wall Street needs the expertise of systems designers, civil engineers, and project managers much more than applied mathematicians cranking out formulas for pricing new derivatives. The financial industry, which created so much mayhem and destruction in the past decade, would once again return to its core vocation of directing the long-term savings of pension and insurance funds into the long-term investments needed for a revival of long-term growth.

3

DECODING THE FEDERAL BUDGET

There is nothing more important for our economic future—or less understood—than the federal budget. It allocates around 20 percent of our national output to such crucial priorities as health, education, science, the environment, and national defense. It determines, to a large extent, how many Americans suffer from poverty and even the level of inequality in incomes. And yet our national debates on economics, and the positions of both Democratic and Republican leaders, obscure more than they reveal about the choices facing the nation.

Here's why. While people have a reasonable sense of their own budgets, they have little sense of how Washington taxes and spends. We may know well what an extra $1,000 might mean for our own standard of living or ability to pay the bills. But what does $1 billion mean at the national level? (Hint: With 320 million Americans, $1 billion is a mere $3 per person). Or what does $1 trillion in infrastructure spending over five years signify? (Hint: With GDP of nearly $20 trillion per year, $1 trillion over five years amounts to roughly 1 percent of national income per year.)

Our starting point is that the fiscal situation of the United States is already precarious. According to the Congressional Budget Office, the budget deficit during the coming decade, should we stick with existing policies, is likely to average around 4 percent of GDP. Increases in spending on infrastructure, public services, or the military would add to a large and rapidly growing stock of debt.

To solve our economic problems, we need to overhaul our understanding of the budget, the role of government, and the nature of fiscal policy. Neither party yet offers a realistic solution. President Obama presided over a slow drip of gradual decline, rising debts, and stagnation. President Trump proposes to boost spending, especially on infrastructure and the military, but also to cut taxes sharply. It doesn't add up, to say the least. Or more accurately, it adds up to a massive and debilitating debt crisis down the road. We will need a better way.

Our starting point should be the pithy observation of former Vice President Joe Biden: "Don't tell me what you value; show me your budget, and I'll tell you what you value." The federal budget is an expression of what we value as a nation because it shows how we choose to allocate our national resources.

Values without a budget are empty words, election promises that are at best naive and, more typically, cynical lies. Obama's "Yes, we can" promises of 2008 failed precisely because there was no long-term budget plan behind them. That was true even when, in 2009 and 2010, Obama had large Democratic Party majorities in both houses of Congress. In fact, Obama's failure to deliver on his uplifting 2008 campaign was baked in from the start, from his very first budget proposals, which failed to call for an increase in federal revenues to pay for increased outlays.

Here, in brief, is how the federal budget works. On the one side we have the revenues raised by federal taxes and, on the other side, the outlays. Federal taxes take in about 18 percent of GDP, mostly from income taxes and payroll taxes (for Medicare and Social Security). Together with state and local taxes, the total tax collection of all levels of government amounts to around 32 percent of GDP. Let's keep that number in mind.

On the federal spending side, we have four main categories. The first is national security. That entails the Pentagon, intelligence agencies, homeland security, the Energy Department's nuclear weapons programs, other international security programs in the State Department, and the Department of Veterans Affairs (the delayed costs of past wars). In total, annual outlays now total around $900 billion per year, or roughly 4.9 percent of GDP.

The second category covers so-called "mandatory" programs, including health (Medicare, Medicaid, other health), Social Security, and income support programs (such as food stamps). These total around 12.6 percent of GDP. Their costs have been rising as a share GDP in recent years because of the aging of the population and the soaring costs of health care. The rising outlays due to aging will, of course, continue.

The third category is interest payments on the government (public) debt. With the ratio of public debt to national income now around 75 percent and the average interest costs on the debt around 2 percentage points per year, the interest charges are around 1.5 percent of GDP. These costs will rise when interest rates return to more normal, higher levels.

The fourth category of spending, sometimes called "non-security discretionary programs," includes the federal government's investments in the future, such as biomedical research, other science and technology, low-carbon energy R&D and deployment, education and job skills, fast rail and other public infrastructure, the courts and penal system, and a small amount (a meager 0.2 percent of GDP) for helping the world's poorest countries to fight hunger, illiteracy, and disease.

The astute reader will have already spotted the problem. Tax revenues total around 18 percent of GDP. Yet outlays for the first three categories (national security, mandatory programs, and interest on the debt) total around 19 percent of GDP! Revenues do not even cover the first three categories, much less the crucial fourth category. Borrowing, rather than tax revenues, must therefore pay for the entire nonsecurity discretionary budget, a dreadful and unsustainable situation.

The simple truth is that America doesn't raise enough tax revenues to finance the key public investments for our future. Instead of investing federal funds adequately in higher education, we pile a trillion dollars of student debt on the backs of our young people. Instead of upgrading our infrastructure, we drive on crumbling highways and bridges. Instead of building a low-carbon energy system, we continue to rely on coal, oil, and gas, endangering the entire planet as a consequence.

President Trump says he will solve these problems, but with what funds? As a candidate, then-Senator Obama said the same in 2008 and ran into a dead end. Instead of investing in our future, Obama has presided over cuts in the nonsecurity discretionary programs, with budget allocations declining from around 2.6 percent of GDP in 2008 (just before Obama came to office) to a meager 2.3 percent of GDP in 2016. The projections are even more ominous, with nonsecurity discretionary spending on a trajectory to decline below 2.0 percent of GDP by around 2020.[1] Crucial federal programs remain on life support as budget outlays for key public investments continue to fall.

What is the way forward if we want to invest in a twenty-first-century future rather than suffer from continued stagnation and decline? Most importantly, we will need to think out of the box. The first strategy should be to cut back on wasted federal outlays. The biggest saving should be on the military side. Despite the reflexive call to boost military spending, we should instead end the perpetual Middle East wars, cut back sharply on America's overseas military bases, and negotiate sharp global limits on nuclear arms rather than invest in a new, costly round of the nuclear arms race. In a later chapter, I will also detail the ways that our nation can save on total health outlays, albeit by shifting part of the today's private health spending onto the federal budget with big offsetting reductions in private health spending.

Significant budget action, however, will have to come on the revenue side. We have refused, since Ronald Reagan became president in 1981, to fund the federal government adequately despite the realities of an aging population and the urgent need to invest in advanced skills, education, infrastructure, and environmental sustainability. Reagan told us in 1981 that government was the problem, not the solution; Democratic Party presidential candidate Walter Mondale got buried in Reagan's 1984 landslide after Mondale said that he'd raise taxes. Since then, both parties have simply denied the need for more revenues built up public debt instead. We are now running on fumes, funding the entire nonsecurity discretionary budget with a bulge in public debt.

For a while, the so-called "progressive" idea was simple: Instead of calling for higher taxes, progressives would proclaim that borrowing was just fine. Paul Krugman told us time and again not to worry about the public debt, that it's actually good for us, by stimulating demand while not adding much to future tax burdens. Many Republican supply-siders said the same, though their spending priorities were typically different (usually calling for more military spending).

That was then. In 2007, the debt-to-GDP ratio was 35 percent; now it's 75 percent. Given current trends and policies, according to the Congressional Budget Office, it will be around 86 percent in 2025, and in 2036 will reach a staggering 110 percent of GDP (figure 3.1).[2] Today interest rates are low; in the future, when they're back to normal, at around 4 percent per annum, the debt burden will hit very hard indeed, requiring at least 3 percent of GDP, if not more, to pay for interest payments.

So how do other countries manage their budgets? Simply, they tax more as a share of national income. The United States

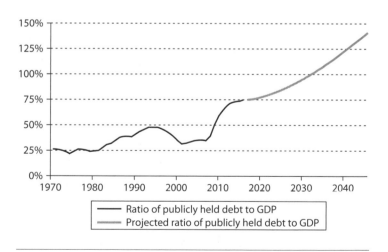

FIGURE 3.1 Long-Term Trend of Public Debt on Unchanged Policies (percent of GDP)

taxes around 32 percent. Canada, with its highly successful public sector programs in health and education, taxes at around 39 percent (and it's still thriving!). The Scandinavian social democracies—Denmark, Norway, and Sweden—tax around 50 percent of GDP. And yes, they get great value for money, with smaller budget deficits, lower debt-to-GDP ratios, at least a month per year of paid vacation, free public health care, free college tuition, guaranteed maternity leave and quality child care, modern infrastructure, and much greener economies.

Despite their higher tax rates (or, more accurately, because of the social services these taxes purchase), the Scandinavian countries and Canada rank much higher than the United States in overall national happiness. In the 2016 rankings of national happiness, the top six countries were Denmark, Switzerland, Iceland, Norway, Finland, and Canada, with the United States coming in thirteenth.[3] All of the top leaders in national happiness collect more in tax revenues as a share of GDP than the United States, thereby paying for an ample array of public investments and public services that contribute to prosperity, greater equality, and higher self-declared happiness.

So how can the United States fund its future and collect more revenues without damaging the incentives to save and invest? Part of the answer lies in ending absurd tax giveaways, like the gimmicks that have allowed Apple Inc. and others to keep their profit stashed abroad in tax havens. Ending corporate abuse could garner around 1 percent of GDP. Another 1–2 percent of GDP could come from wealth and income taxes on the super rich.

Yet, as in Scandinavia, I would also recommend a value-added tax (like a national sales tax), enough to raise another 3–4 percent of national income. The total federal revenues would thereby reach around 24 percent of GDP and around

38 percent for combined federal, state, and local government. This would be roughly equivalent with Canada and still well below the revenues of northern Europe. At least the United States would be in a position to think about investing in our future once again.

As a candidate, Trump seemed to suggest most of the infrastructure scale-up, and his stated desire for increased military outlays, could be paid for with more debt. Pursuing this as president would be a mistake, a major burden on the future, and one that would likely fizzle out in a fiscal crisis at the end of a populist boom in spending. Part of the infrastructure spending can indeed be financed by public debt (especially for infrastructure that will directly generate future tax revenues), but not all of it, especially when the baseline trajectory of public debt is so ominous.

Republicans are looking for cuts in the corporate tax rate in order to keep American-based companies competitive with international companies. There may be some merit to cutting the top corporate tax rate if combined with an end to corporate loopholes and the foreign tax deferral provisions. But the more basic deal should be to combine any corporate tax reform with the introduction of a VAT or similar tax (such as a progressive consumption tax) in order to ensure that total revenues relative to GDP are increased adequately to cover future needs.

Such ideas are currently outside of the political mainstream, but I believe that they will return to the center of national politics as the American people realize that both parties are shortchanging their futures. Senator Bernie Sanders ran his campaign on mobilizing vastly more revenues for much greater public investments. He decisively rallied the young. I believe that this message will soon come to the fore of our national politics more generally; it is vital for our economic future.

4

SUSTAINABLE INFRASTRUCTURE AFTER THE AUTOMOBILE AGE

The breakthrough American infrastructure of the early nineteenth century was the Erie Canal, which connected the Midwest farm belt with the Port of New York and the eastern seaboard. In the second half of the nineteenth century, the railroad offered the next infrastructure revolution by connecting the two oceans and the continent in between. In the middle of the last century, the transformational infrastructure was the interstate highway system, consummating America's twentieth-century love affair with the automobile.

Each new wave of infrastructure underpinned a half-century of economic growth. Yet each wave of infrastructure also reached its inherent limits, in part by causing adverse side effects such as pollution, congestion, or new inequalities of income and status, and in part by being overtaken by a new technological revolution. And so it will be with our generation.

Our job is to renew our infrastructure in line with new needs, especially climate safety, and new opportunities, especially ubiquitous online information and smart machines. The UN's Sustainable Development Goal 9 (Target 9.1) calls on all countries to "Develop quality, reliable, sustainable and resilient infrastructure, including regional and transborder infrastructure, to support economic development and human well-being, with a focus on affordable and equitable access for all."

Our generation also needs to reinvest in infrastructure for another very basic reason. The nation's core infrastructure—its highways, power grid, water treatment and waste systems—is now at least a half-century old, and much of it is falling into disrepair. The American Society of Civil Engineers estimates that we need around $3 trillion in infrastructure investments during the coming decade in order to upgrade the old and failing capital stock.[1] The group estimates that we have funding for around half that sum, with a looming $1.4 trillion financing gap to be filled.

The chronic underinvestment in infrastructure dates back at least thirty years, essentially since the completion of the interstate highway system. Starting in the early 1980s, under the Reagan administration, public spending on just water and transport infrastructure fell from around 1 percent of GDP to around 0.6 percent of GDP, as shown in figure 4.1.

Instead of building new cutting-edge infrastructure, we began merely to patch the existing system. We've done that now for more than three decades. But with the advanced age of the existing infrastructure, patching alone will no longer suffice; we need a more fundamental overhaul.

In an era when the two major parties agree on almost nothing, there is an emerging consensus on the need to spend more on infrastructure. In the 2016 campaign, Hillary Clinton called for $275 billion in new infrastructure spending over the coming five years. Donald Trump replied that $275 billion was insufficient, and both he and Bernie Sanders campaigned for $1 trillion of infrastructure investments. While campaign positions are wish lists, not policies, in this case they seem

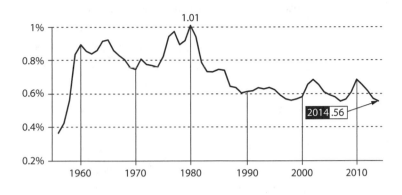

FIGURE 4.1 Federal Investments on Transport
and Water as Percent of GDP

to signal a realization that the era of patch-patch-patch has reached the end.

There has been much less discussion, however, about where and how to spend the funds. The Obama administration offers a case study in how not to decide those issues. Obama made one attempt to increase infrastructure spending, as part of the 2009 stimulus spending in his first term. But that 2009 stimulus package was designed all wrong from the point of view of making high-quality public investments. The stimulus spending was aimed at quick job creation rather than long-term transformation. The administration's favorite buzz phrase, remember, was "shovel-ready projects," recalling the labor-intensive public works spending of the New Deal, in the Great Depression, rather than the advanced technological needs of the twenty-first century. As a result, Obama produced few if any lasting results in the area of infrastructure. Despite years of bold talk about high-speed rail, for example, not a single mile of high-speed rail was laid.

I propose the opposite approach to short-term "stimulus." I'd call it "long-term thinking," even "long-term planning" (to use an idea that is anathema in Washington). Rather than trying to deploy construction workers within the next sixty days, I propose that we envision the kind of built environment we want for the next sixty years. With a shared vision of America's infrastructure goals, actually designing and building the new transport, energy, communications, and water systems will surely require at least a generation, just as the interstate highway system did a half-century ago. The interstate highway system was given legislative mandate in the 1956 Federal Highway Aid Act, under President Eisenhower, and the actual construction of the system stretched through the Kennedy, Johnson, Nixon, Ford, and Carter presidencies, in a bipartisan effort lasting a quarter-century.

The new vision should start with a basic realization: The Age of the Automobile is drawing to a close. Yes, cars will still be with us, but never again as centrally in our lives, economy, and culture. We will share them rather than own them individually; we will favor new urban patterns that promote walking, cycling, and other ways to stay healthy; we will enjoy new options for public transportation; and of course we will interact more through virtual means, such as the now ubiquitous videoconferences rather than conferences in person.

The era of the internal combustion engine is also drawing to an end, to be replaced by climate-friendly electric vehicles and other forms of low-carbon mobility. American households will no longer aspire to own two cars in every garage, but instead will have mobility apps on every phone, to hail self-driving vehicles that they will share rather than own. In high-density cities, the overall number of vehicles will fall considerably, while the intensity of their use (passenger trips per day) will soar. Low-income households will likely reap enormous advantages in improved access to transport services, similar to the gains in access to low-cost mobile phone services.

The first infrastructure task, therefore, is one of imagination. What kind of cities and rural areas do we seek in the future? What kind of infrastructure should underpin that vision? And who should plan, develop, build, finance, and operate the systems? These are the real choices facing us, though they've hardly been considered in our political debates to date. My best guesses at answering these questions are the following:

We should seek an infrastructure that abides by the triple bottom line of sustainable development. That is, the networks of roads, power, water, and communications should support economic prosperity, social fairness, and environmental sustainability. The triple bottom line will in turn push us to adopt three guiding principles.

First, the infrastructure should be "smart," deploying state-of-the-art information and communications technologies and new nanotechnologies to achieve a high efficiency of resource use, such as the new carbon fibers for lightweight vehicles.

Second, the infrastructure should be shared and accessible to all, whether as shared vehicles, open-access broadband in public areas, or shared green spaces in cities.

Third, transport infrastructure should promote public health and environmental safety. The new transport systems should not only shift to electrical vehicles and other zero-emission vehicles but should also promote much more walking, bicycling, and public transport use. Power generation should shift decisively to zero-carbon primary energy sources, such as wind, solar, hydro, and nuclear power. The built environment should be resilient to rising ocean levels, higher temperatures, more intense heat waves, and more extreme storms.

Here's the rub. Markets alone can't come close to achieving these goals. Infrastructure requires fundamental choices on land use. In the twentieth century, for example, conscious decisions by mayors, governors, and Congress (backed, of course, by the intense lobbying of big oil and the auto industry) opted to use urban land for roads and highways rather than trolleys and light rail. Now we need conscious decisions to opt out of carbon-based energy and transport systems in favor of clean energy and electrification.

In the northeast United States, for example, decarbonization probably entails teaming up with Canada to bring far more Quebec hydropower down from regions near the Hudson Bay in an expanded transmission system. Such a strategy requires long-term purchase agreements between end users and the hydropower providers, as well as complex public rights of way in both Canada and the United States, involving several U.S. states. In short, a binational program for low-carbon hydropower in the U.S. and Canadian northeast would be a major public policy decision involving multiple actors, including major cities (e.g., Boston and New York), several states, the regional grid operators and utility regulators, and the two national governments.

I recently helped lead a project on "deep decarbonization" for the world's major emitting countries, including the United States.[2] To achieve the goal set in the Paris climate agreement of staying "well below 2 degrees C" (or 3.6 degrees F) in global warming, all countries will need to build low-carbon infrastructure. Our project examined, and verified, the technological and economic feasibility of decarbonization. We showed that the new infrastructure must be based on three low-carbon pillars: high end-use efficiency of energy (such as through smart grids and smart appliances); zero-carbon power generation (wind, solar, hydro, nuclear, biofuels); and fuel switching from internal combustion engines to electric vehicles, and from boilers burning heating oil to heat pumps run on electricity. We also demonstrated a feasible, low-cost pathway of deep decarbonization for the U.S. economy, with the shift in power generation to low-carbon sources, as shown in figure 4.2.

Yet we also found the essential need for long-term planning and strong cooperation among neighboring countries and between national and local governments. There is nothing "shovel ready" about decarbonization. The challenge combines the technological complexity of the moon shot and the organizational complexity of building the interstate highway system.

Once we agree on the general direction, we should give wide berth to, and financial incentives for, local innovation. Consider the experiment that began in September 2016 in Pittsburgh. The city government is teaming up with Uber and with Carnegie Mellon University, a world leader in information sciences, to introduce self-driving shared mobility services. I have little doubt that this powerhouse combination will make important breakthroughs and will be widely emulated by cities across the country. My confidence is bolstered by the fact that electric vehicle–based shared driving fits all of the objectives of sustainable development: efficiency of vehicle use (cutting down sharply on vehicles per person), high social access through the sharing economy, and environmental sustainability.

One of the important reasons for our national slow economic growth is that private investors are waiting on the

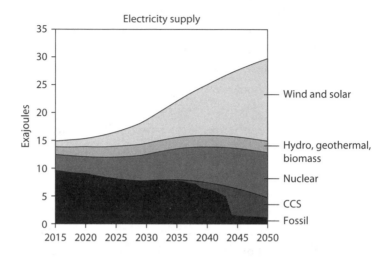

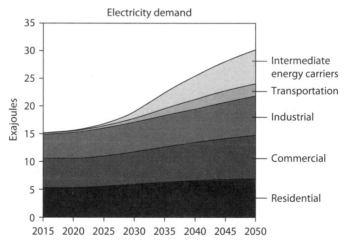

FIGURE 4.2 Path to Low-Carbon Electricity in the United States

sidelines until basic infrastructure decisions are made at the national level. With public investment held back by chronic underfunding and the lack of a shared national vision, private investment inevitably is held back as well. Will we partner with Canada on more hydropower? Will we shift decisively to electric vehicles? Will we reinvest in nuclear energy or close the industry? Will we invest in new interstate power transmission lines to bring low-cost renewable energy to population centers? Will we finally build high-speed intercity rail? Will we rebuild the infrastructure to promote high-density, socially inclusive, low-carbon urban living? Will we build smart grids to support autonomous vehicles, energy efficiency, and the like? Clear public policy answers in the affirmative will greatly boost private investment opportunities.

But who is to plan these systems? In China, which has successfully installed more than 20,000 kilometers of high-speed rail (speeds greater than 200 km/h), the National Development and Reform Commission helps to amalgamate investment priorities and to organize financing for the country's vast infrastructure needs. America's infrastructure planning processes will of course be very different, with far more engagement from citizens, local governments, think tanks, and the courts as well, to uphold regulatory standards and processes. Yet we do need a national process to get things moving.

I propose that President Trump and the new Congress quickly establish a national commission on twenty-first-century infrastructure, including members of Congress, executive branch departments and agencies, state and local government representatives, the National Academy of Engineering, and academia, private business, and civil society, to put before the nation a compelling vision of a smart, inclusive, and environmentally sustainable infrastructure. This commission should report back to Congress, the president, and the American people within one year. Congress could act on the recommendations in 2018, time enough to build an effort that will in fact last several decades.

Last, but not least, must come the trillions of dollars over several decades needed to implement such a plan. The multiple sources of public revenues are clear: taxes on fossil fuels, user fees, general government revenues, bond issues, taxes on land improvements, public leasing and royalties, and private project financing. With regard to the vast needs for private capital, Wall Street should take a new, socially constructive role that goes far beyond high-frequency trading and peddling toxic assets. As America builds the new infrastructure for the age of sustainable development, Wall Street would then also restore its role as the financial powerhouse behind the world's most dynamic economy.

5

FACING UP TO INCOME INEQUALITY

I n 2016, the census bureau announced a heartening 5 percent gain in the median household income between 2014 and 2015, the largest one-year gain on record. Yet a look at the longer-term trends offers a sobering perspective.[1] The jump in household income merely helps to make up for lost ground; the median earnings in 2015 were actually lower than back in 1999—sixteen years earlier.

While household median incomes have stagnated since the late 1990s, the inflation-adjusted earnings of poorer households have been stagnant for even longer, roughly forty years. Meanwhile, households at or near the top of the income distribution have enjoyed sizable increases in living standards.[2] The result is a stark widening of the gap between rich and poor households. Clearly those left behind fueled the campaigns of both Donald Trump and Bernie Sanders.

In the dramatic widening of income inequality, America is not alone. Many countries, rich and poor alike, have experienced a significant widening of inequality in recent decades. The issue of high and rising inequality is so vital to social wellbeing that the UN member states adopted Sustainable Development Goal 10 to "reduce inequality within and among countries," the first time that the fight against inequality was given such prominence by all UN member states.

Indeed, there is perhaps no issue in America more contentious than income inequality. Everybody has a theory as to why the gap between rich and poor has grown and what—if anything—should be done to close it. A full explanation can help explain why the United States stands out for having an especially high and rising inequality of income.

There are three main factors at play: technology, trade, and politics. Technological innovations have raised the demand for highly trained workers, thereby pushing up the incomes of college-educated workers relative to high school–educated workers. Global trade has exposed the wages of industrial workers to tough international competition from workers at much lower pay scales. And our federal politics has tended, during the past thirty-five years, to weaken the political role of the working class, diminish union bargaining power, and cap or cut the government benefits received by working-class families.

Consider technology. Throughout modern history, ingenious machines have been invented to replace heavy physical labor. This has been hugely beneficial: Most (though not all) American workers have been lucky to escape the hard toil, dangers, and diseases of heavy farm work, mining, and heavy industry. Farm jobs have been lost, but, with some exceptions, their backbreaking drudgery has been transformed into office jobs. Farmworkers and miners combined now account for less than 1 percent of the labor force.

Yet the office jobs required more skills than the farm jobs that disappeared. The new office jobs needed a high school education, and, more recently, a college degree. So who benefited? Middle-class and upper-class kids fortunate enough to receive the education and skills for the new office jobs. And who lost? Mostly poorer kids who couldn't afford the education to meet the rising demands for skilled work.

Now the race between education and technology has again heated up. The machines are getting smarter, faster than ever before—indeed, faster than countless households can help their kids to stay in the job market. Sure, there are still good jobs available, as long as you've graduated with a degree in computer science from MIT, or at least a nod in that direction.

Globalization is closely related to technology and, indeed, is made possible by it. It has a similar effect, of squeezing incomes of lower-skilled workers. Not only are the assembly-line robots competing for American jobs; so too are the lower-wage workers half a world away from the United States. American workers in so-called "traded goods" sectors, meaning the sectors in direct competition with imports, have therefore faced an additional whammy of intense downward pressure on wages.

For a long time, economists resisted the public's concern about trade depressing wages of lower-skilled workers. Twenty-two years ago I coauthored a paper arguing that rising trade with China and other low-wage countries was squeezing the earnings of America's lower-skilled workers.[3] The paper was met with skepticism. A generation later, the economics profession has mostly come around to recognizing that globalization is a culprit in the rise of income inequality. This doesn't mean that global trade should be ended, since trade does indeed expand the overall economy. It does, however, suggest that open trade should be accompanied by policies to improve the lot of lower-wage, lower-skilled workers, especially those directly hit by global trade, but also those indirectly affected.

Many analyses of rising income inequality stop at this point, emphasizing the twin roles of technology and trade, and perhaps debating their relative importance. Yet the third part of the story—the role of politics—is perhaps the most vital of all. Politics shows up in two ways. First, politics helps to determine the bargaining power of workers versus corporations: how the overall pie is divided between capital and labor. Second, politics determines whether the federal budget is used to spread the benefits of a rising economy to the workers and households left behind.

Unfortunately, U.S. politics has tended to put the government's muscle on the side of big business and against the working class. Remember the Reagan revolution: tax cuts for the rich and the companies, and union busting for the workers? Remember the Bill Clinton program to "end welfare as we know it," a program that pushed poor and working-class moms into long-distance commuting for desperately low wages, while their kids were often left back in dangerous and squalid conditions? Remember the case of the federal minimum wage, which has been kept so low for so long by Congress that its inflation-adjusted value peaked in 1968?

There is no deep mystery as to why federal politics has turned its back on the poor and the working class. The political system has become "pay to play," with the 2016 federal election cycle costing around $7 billion, largely financed by the well-heeled class in the Hamptons and the C-suites of Wall Street and Big Oil, certainly not the little guy on unemployment benefits. As the insightful political scientist Martin Gilens has persuasively shown, when it comes to federal public policy, only the views of the rich actually have sway in Washington.

So in the end, the inequality of income in the United States is high and rising while in other countries facing the same technological and trade forces, the inequality remains lower and the rise in inequality hasn't been so stark. What explains the difference in outcomes? In the other countries, democratic politics offers voice and representation to average voters rather than to the rich. Votes and voters matter more than dollars.

To delve more deeply into the comparison between the United States and other countries, it is useful to measure the inequality of income in each country in two different ways. The first way measures the inequality of "market incomes" of households—that is, the income of households measured before taxes and government benefits are taken into account. The second measures the inequality of "disposable income," taking into account the taxes paid and transfers received by households.

The difference between the two measures shows the extent of income redistribution achieved through government taxation and spending. In all of the high-income countries, the inequality of market income is greater than the inequality of disposable income. The taxes paid by the relatively rich and the transfers made to the relatively poor help to offset some of the inequality of the marketplace.

Figure 5.1 offers just this comparison for the high-income countries. For each country, two measures of inequality based on the "Gini coefficient" are calculated. The Gini coefficient is a measure of income inequality that varies between 0 (full income equality across households) and 1 (full income inequality, in which one household has all of the income). Countries as a whole tend to have a Gini coefficient of disposable income somewhere between 0.25 (low inequality) and 0.60 (very high inequality).

In the figure, we see the two values of the Gini coefficient for each country: a higher value (more inequality) based on market income and a lower value (less inequality) based on

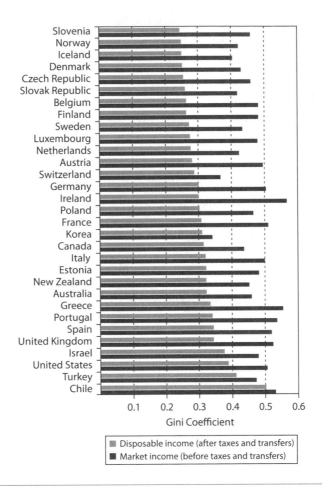

FIGURE 5.1 Measuring Income Inequality

disposable income (that is, after taxes and transfers). We can see that in every country, the tax-and-transfer system shifts at least some income from the rich to the poor, thereby pushing down the Gini coefficient. Yet the amount of net redistribution is very different in different countries and is especially low in the United States.

Compare, for example, the United States and Denmark. In the United States, the Gini coefficient on market income is a very high 0.51, and on disposable income, 0.40, still quite high. In Denmark, by comparison, the Gini coefficient on market income is a bit lower than the United States, at 0.43. Yet Denmark's Gini coefficient on disposable income is far lower, only 0.25. America's tax-and-transfer system reduces the Gini coefficient by only 0.11. Denmark's tax-and-transfer system reduces the Gini coefficient by 0.18, half again as much as in the United States.

How does Denmark end up with so much lower inequality of disposable income? The answer is in its budget policies. Denmark taxes more heavily than the United States and uses the greater tax revenue to provide free health care, child care, sick leave, maternity and paternity leave, guaranteed vacations, free university tuition, early childhood programs, and much more. Denmark taxes a hefty 51 percent of national income and provides a robust range of high-quality public services. The United States taxes a far lower 32 percent and offers a rickety social safety net. In the United States, people are left to sink or swim. Many sink.

So, many Americans would suspect, Denmark's citizens are miserable and being crushed by taxes, right? Well, not so right. Denmark actually comes out number one in the world happiness rankings, while the United States comes in thirteenth. Denmark's life expectancy is also higher, its poverty lower, and its citizens' trust in government and in each other vastly higher than in the United States.

Herein lies a key lesson for the United States. America's inequality of disposable income is the highest among the rich countries. America is paying a heavy price in lost well-being for its high and rising inequality of income, and for its failure to shift more benefits to the poor and working class.

We have become a country with a huge distrust of government and of each other; we have become a country with a huge underclass of people who can't afford their prescription drugs, tuition payments, or rent or mortgage payments. Despite a roughly threefold increase in national income per person over the past fifty years, Americans report to survey takers no higher level of happiness than they did back in 1960. The fraying of America's social ties, the increased loneliness and distrust, eats away at the American dream and the American spirit. It's even contributing to a rise in the death rates among middle-aged, white, non-Hispanic Americans, a shocking recent reversal of very long-term trends of rising longevity. (I'll explore this issue further in chapter 8.)

The current trends will tend to get even worse unless and until American politics changes direction. As I will describe in chapter 6, the coming generation of yet smarter machines and robots will claim additional jobs among the lower-skilled workers and those performing rote activities. Wages will be pushed lower except for those with higher training and skills. Capital owners (who will own the robots and the software systems to operate them) will reap large profits while many young people will be unable to find gainful employment. The advance in technology could thereby contribute to a further downward spiral in social cohesion.

That is, unless we decide to do things differently. Twenty-eight countries in the Organization for Economic Cooperation and Development (OECD) have lower inequality of disposable income than the United States, even though these countries share the same technologies and compete in the same global marketplace as the United States. These income comparisons underscore that America's high inequality is a choice, not an irreversible law of the modern world economy.

6

SMART MACHINES AND
THE FUTURE OF JOBS

S ince the early 1800s, several waves of technological change have transformed how we work and live. Each new technological marvel—the steam engine, railroad, ocean steamship, telegraph, harvester, automobile, radio, airplane, TV, computer, satellite, mobile phone, and now the Internet—has changed our home lives, communities, workplaces, schools, and leisure time. For two centuries, we've asked whether ever more powerful machines would free us from drudgery or would instead enslave us.

The question is becoming urgent. IBM's Deep Blue and other chess-playing computers now routinely beat the world's chess champions. Google's DeepMind defeated the European Go champion late last year. IBM's Watson has gone from becoming the world's *Jeopardy* champion to becoming an expert medical diagnostician. Self-driving cars on the streets of Pittsburgh are on the verge of displacing Uber drivers. And Baxter, the industrial robot, is carrying out an expanding range of assembly-line and warehouse operations. Will the coming generations of smart machines deliver us leisure and well-being or joblessness and falling wages?

The answer to this question is not simple. There is neither a consensus nor deep understanding of the future of jobs in an economy increasingly built on smart machines. The machines have gotten much smarter so fast that their implications for the future of work, home life, schooling, and leisure are a matter of open speculation.

We need to pursue policies that ensure the coming generation of smart machines works for us and our well-being, rather than our working for the machines and the few who control their operating systems. As with other major challenges of sustainable development, America is not alone regarding the jobs crisis. The challenge is certainly being felt worldwide. Sustainable Development Goal 8 indeed calls for "full and productive employment and decent work for all."

In a way, the economic effects of smarter machines are akin to the economic effects of international trade. Trade expands the nation's economic pie but also changes how the pie is divided. Smart machines do the same. In the past, smarter machines have expanded the economic pie and shifted jobs and earnings away from low-skilled workers to high-skilled workers. In the future, robots and artificial intelligence are likely to shift national income from all types of workers toward capitalists and from the young to the old.

Consider England's Industrial Revolution in the first part of the nineteenth century, when James Watt's steam engine, the mechanization of textile production, and the railroad created the first industrial society. No doubt the economic pie expanded remarkably. England's national income roughly doubled from 1820 to 1860. Yet traditional weavers were thrown out of their jobs; the Luddites, an early movement of English workers, tried to smash the machines that were impoverishing them; and poet William Blake wrote of the "dark Satanic mills" of the new industrial society. An enlarging economic pie, yes; a new prosperity shared by all, decidedly not.

Looking back at two centuries of more and more powerful machines (and the accompanying technologies and systems to operate them), we can see one overarching truth: Technological advances made the society much richer but also continually reshuffled the winners and losers. Similarly, one overarching pattern was repeatedly replayed. The march of technology has favored those with more education and training. Smart machines require well-trained specialists to operate them. An expanded economic pie favors those with managerial and professional skills who can navigate the complexities of finance, administration, management, and technological systems.

Overall, better machines caused national income to soar and the man-hours spent in hard physical labor to decline markedly. Seventy-hour workweeks in 1870 have become thirty-five-hour workweeks today. An average of around six years of schooling has become an average of seventeen years.[1] With increasing longevity, most workers can now look forward to fifteen years or more of retirement, an idea simply unimaginable in the late nineteenth century. It's amazing to reflect that for Americans fifteen years and over, the average time at work each day is now just 3 hours 11 minutes.[2] Those at work average 7 hours 34 minutes, but only 42.1 percent of Americans fifteen and over are at work on an average day. The rest of the time, other than sleep and personal care, is taken up with schooling, retirement, caring for children, leisure and sports, shopping, and household activities.

Smart machines in the nineteenth century provided massive power (the steam engine), transport (rail, steamships, automobiles), information (telegraph), and material transformation (steel and textile mills), and also, crucially, a more and more powerful substitute for human brawn—that is, backbreaking physical labor—on the farm and in the mines. Seed drills, cotton gins, threshers, reapers, combined harvesters, and by the early twentieth century, tractors, not only opened up vast new farmlands but also replaced millions of farmworkers by machines. Mechanical cotton pickers in the early decades of the twentieth century displaced millions of African American sharecroppers on southern farms and contributed to the great African American migration to northern cities.

Hard physical labor declined as machines did more and more of this work; but so too did jobs and earnings for lower-skilled workers. Those lucky enough to get an education could obtain the higher skills needed for the new jobs. Those who could not suffered stagnant or falling wages and a further loss of social status. In the past two decades, more and more low-skilled men have simply dropped out of the labor force entirely.

The most important policy response is to ensure that students stay in school long enough to achieve the skills they need for the new and better jobs. As long as the national supply of skilled workers roughly keeps pace with the rising demand for skilled workers, while the supply of low-skilled workers declines in line with the decline in the numbers of low-skilled jobs, the gap in earnings between high- and low-skilled workers remains relatively stable. In this way, the rising school attainments of Americans during the twentieth century roughly maintained a balance with the shift from low-skilled work to high-skilled work.[3]

Yet after around 1980, the earnings of highly educated workers (notably, those with bachelor's degrees and higher) increased sharply relative to less educated workers (those with a high school diploma or less). Greater international trade and offshoring probably had a role in this, and so did technology, with smarter machines replacing high school–educated workers in a widening range of manual and repetitive tasks. The shift of the labor force toward higher-skilled workers wasn't fast enough in recent decades. Many American lower-skilled workers have been hit hard by lost jobs and falling wages.

Today's smart machines are replacing not just brawn but also brains. The futurist Ray Kurzweil and others have popularized the term "singularity" to mean a time in the near future when machines are simply better than humans at just about everything: moving, assembling, driving, writing, calculating, war making, teaching (bad news for me!), and the rest.

Several recent studies, including at Oxford University and McKinsey, have tried to estimate the share of jobs that are likely to be up for grabs by smart machines in the next twenty or so years.[4] Each occupation is analyzed for the kinds of tasks needed. Are they highly repetitive or highly context specific? Do they require highly specialized mechanical skills, a high degree of interaction with others, or a high measure of emotional empathy? And so on. From this categorization of job tasks, the researchers estimate the share of jobs that can be substituted by robots and artificial intelligence systems. Their answer: Roughly half of today's jobs are susceptible to at least some kinds of replacement by smart machines.

The implications are a bit tricky. On the one hand, smarter machines mean more economic output and, in principle, a larger economic pie to share among the American people. Investing in machines, or in the companies that produce the smart systems that run them, would seem to offer high returns; capital owners would be very likely to benefit. On the other hand, smarter machines could mean a decline in the demand for workers. Young people with labor to sell but little wealth to invest could find themselves on the short end of the economic stick, with lower wages and no grand prospect of benefiting from the higher returns to capital. Older and richer Americans would tend to benefit, younger and poorer Americans would tend to fall behind.

This would not be the end of the story, however. If today's young people find themselves without jobs, they not only will be poorer, but will also save less as a result of shrunken incomes. Yes, the smarter machines will offer a higher return to saving, but the supply of national saving will shrink. A careful theoretical analysis reveals a stark truth: Smart machines could actually set in motion a downward spiral, wherein today's young workers can't find decent jobs, and thereby cut back on their saving, which in turn leaves the following generation of young workers even worse off.

This is indeed a frightening vision. And yet the same analysis suggests a way out. If the rich capital owners transfer some of their windfall profits to the struggling young workers, then both the old rich and the young poor would be better off with the smart machines than without them. In effect, the rich older shareholders would compensate the poor younger workers in order to offset the fall in wages.

There are two ways this "offset" could happen. Within families, parents could transfer some of their increased wealth to their children; but alas, that is a solution that is likely to be relevant mainly for richer households.

For the nonrich, the real solution could and should be achieved through fiscal policy. Rich older shareholders should be taxed in order to make transfer payments to the poorer, young workers.

Such transfer payments could be carried out in many ways: a cut in payroll taxes, tuition-free higher education, an expansion of the earned income tax credit (EITC) for low-wage workers, or a "reverse" Social Security system with payments from the old to the young. One policy that has been suggested is a capital grant to every newborn, financed by a wealth tax. In essence, each newborn would receive a robot (or financial claim to one) at birth.

The new age of smart machines has already seen a shift in national income away from wages and toward profits. In automobile manufacturing, for example, where robots have already displaced many assembly-line workers, the share of wage compensation in the industry's value added has tumbled from 57 percent in 1997 to 47 percent in 2014. For the economy as a whole, a recent study reports a decline in the labor share of national income from around 68 percent in 1947 to 60 percent in 2013. The shift toward capital income seems to be well underway and is likely a key factor in America's sharply higher inequality of income. As machines become even smarter in future years, the economy-wide shift from wage income to profit income is likely to continue.

In addition to income redistribution from capital owners to workers (and from old to young) there are three other steps we should plan to take.

First, as old jobs disappear and new ones are created, we should emulate Germany's successful apprenticeship programs, which train young workers in the skills needed in the economy. The President's Council of Economic Advisers has rightly emphasized the need for scaling up this kind of active training.[5]

Second, we should prepare for a workforce in which workers will change jobs with much greater frequency than in the past. In an age of disruptive technology, we should plan for disruption. Changing jobs should be regarded as normal, training and skill upgrading should be lifelong, and health care and other benefits should follow workers, not jobs.

Third, and finally, let us remember that ever smarter machines could enable us to enjoy much more leisure time and more hours of the day at valuable but nonremunerated activities and volunteer work.

Suppose that singularity indeed arrives, so that robots and expert systems really do perform all the unpleasant and humdrum work of the economy. As long as fiscal policies ensure that everybody, young and old, can share in the bounty, the results could be a twenty-first-century society in which we have much more time—and take more time—to learn, study, create, innovate, and enjoy and protect nature and each other.

7

THE TRUTH ABOUT TRADE

The debate over global trade and investment played a central role throughout the 2016 campaign, as it did in the 1992 election. Back then, third-party candidate Ross Perot claimed that the proposed North American Free Trade Agreement with Canada and Mexico would cause a "giant sucking sound" of jobs out of the United States to low-wage Mexico. Now the debate is over two similar negotiations, the Trans-Pacific Partnership with Asian countries and the Trans-Atlantic Trade and Investment Partnership with Europe.

Both Hillary Clinton and Donald Trump came out against the proposed trade agreements in their current form, as had Bernie Sanders strongly during the Democratic primary race. The Democratic Party platform emphasized opposition to key parts of the TPP. Yet so strong was the corporate lobby that Barack Obama nonetheless proposed pushing TPP through the lame-duck session of Congress after the November election in 2016, until Trump's victory killed that idea. Both the Democratic and Republican mainstream politicians have been strong defenders of globalization without too much concern about the adverse consequences for many Americans. Trump's electoral victory was dependent in part on tapping that anti-trade sentiment, especially in the Rust Belt of the American Midwest.

I am a believer in expanded international trade, but I am an opponent of TPP and TTIP in their current form and political context. This isn't a contradiction, but a reflection of two important realities. First, the proposed treaties are more than trade agreements. They would also establish many important rules of the economy beyond trade and, in fact, would give far too much power to large multinational companies, the corporations whose lobbyists have helped to draft the agreements. Second, trade policy should not be crafted in isolation from related budget measures that would ensure the fairness of economic outcomes. Open trade is broadly beneficial only when combined with smart and fair budget policies. Alas, the United States does not yet have in place the fiscal policies that are needed to make new trade agreements broadly beneficial across the society.

To keep a scorecard on TPP, TTIP, and related trade policy measures, it's important to keep track of four components of international economics. The first is trade in goods and services, when the United States exports or imports merchandise (like coffee) or services (like shipping). The second is the movement of capital, such as when General Motors opens a subsidiary to manufacture parts in Mexico. The third is offshoring of jobs, such as when Apple contracts with the Taiwanese company Foxconn to assemble iPhones in China. And the fourth is global regulatory policies, such as the terms of patents and copyrights. Modern trade agreements are not just about trade; they include all four parts of the international economic system.

When it comes to trade, there are two key concepts to keep in mind. The first is efficiency, meaning the size of the economic pie (or GDP). The second is distribution, meaning how the economic pie is divided between capital and labor, and among different groups of workers (mainly those with college degrees, or higher, versus the rest).

The first major point about expanding U.S. trade with lower-wage countries is that it tends to improve efficiency—enlarge the pie—but also to redistribute the U.S. economic pie toward capital and highly educated workers and away from workers, especially less educated ones. For capitalists and highly educated workers, greater international trade is a no-brainer, a very good thing indeed. For less educated workers, it can be a curse, pushing down wages and pushing some lower-skilled workers out of the labor force entirely.

The second major point about expanded trade is that the gains to the winners are usually large enough to compensate the losers. By taxing the gains from trade accruing to the capitalists and highly educated workers, the federal government could transfer some of the expanded "pie" to America's less educated workers (for example, through an expanded Earned Income Tax Credit). The net result would be that all groups—the capitalists, highly educated workers, and less educated workers—would be better off with more trade, after taking into account the taxes and transfers.

The potential for expanded trade to benefit all parts of the economy—as long as winners compensate losers—is built into the Sustainable Development Goals, which embrace the potentially beneficial effects of an open global trading system. SDG 17 (Target 17.10) indeed calls for "a universal, rules-based, open, non-discriminatory and equitable multilateral trading system under the World Trade Organization."

Here is a numerical example in the U.S. context. Suppose that the U.S. GDP is $18 trillion, divided as $8 trillion for capitalists, $5 trillion for highly educated workers, and $5 trillion for less educated workers. Now suppose that international trade is expanded through a new trade agreement with several developing countries. Because of the efficiency gains from expanded trade, the U.S. GDP increases in this example to $20 trillion (a larger pie), but now is divided as $10 trillion for capitalists, $7 trillion for highly educated workers, and only $3 trillion for less educated workers.

In this example, trade increases the pie and shifts U.S. national income toward capitalists and highly educated workers. The U.S. Chamber of Commerce obviously would like such a trade deal, as would highly educated professionals. At the same time, less educated workers would rightly oppose the trade deal. Yet rather than rail against China or developing countries, the low-skilled workers would do better to recognize that it is their own countrymen, the capitalists and professionals, who have "walked off with the prize" from the trade deal.

So is more trade a good thing or a bad thing? It depends on whose point of view we are considering.

A vote for expanded trade can be made unanimous if the winners are also taxed modestly to help compensate the losers. Continuing with our example, consider a federal tax surcharge—an extra tax—of $1.25 trillion on capitalists, and $1.25 trillion on highly educated workers. The combined tax proceeds, $2.5 trillion, are then distributed to the less educated workers. If we consider incomes after taxes and transfers, the capitalists end up with $8.75 trillion, the highly educated workers with $5.75 trillion, and the less educated workers with $5.5 trillion. Every group now is better off with expanded trade, once the trade is combined with the tax and transfer system.

The conclusion, backed by economic theory and recent history, is that America's trade with lower-wage countries expands U.S. national income but leaves some of America's less educated workers worse off unless the winners compensate the losers. Economists tend to emphasize the first point but too often downplay or simply don't care about the second.

Donald Trump vigorously opposes the proposed trade agreements on the premise that America as a whole has lost from open trade while China and Mexico have won. This "us-versus-them" view is not correct. Trump is correct that many U.S. workers have lost from trade, but he should understand more clearly that American companies and capitalists have won big. The real goal is therefore not to end trade with China, much less to get into a trade war, but to ensure that the gains from trade enjoyed by U.S. capitalists and multinational companies are more fairly and widely shared with the workers, mainly by taxing the corporate profits and redistributing the proceeds to workers through transfer payments (such as the Earned Income Tax Credit), training programs, and other social support programs.

The politically surprising reality is that President Obama championed a further expansion of trade with Asia and Europe without securing any agreement on further compensation of lower-skilled workers, even after thirty-five years of stagnant incomes of lower-skilled workers. These workers have now rebelled—especially the many white, working-class workers who joined Trump's corner—and Clinton scrambled somewhat unconvincingly to oppose TPP and TTIP.

Twenty-five years ago, I supported NAFTA because I believed that Congress and the president would provide the needed compensation for those workers left behind. My change of heart about trade agreements more recently— leading to my opposition to TPP and TTIP—flows heavily from the sad fact that neither the Republican-led Congress nor Democratic Party presidents (Bill Clinton and Barack Obama) have done much of anything to ensure that the benefits of trade are widely shared within the United States. American politics tends not to compensate the losers, but rather tries to ignore them.

The downside for American workers has been greatly exacerbated by the second and third components of the international economy: increased capital flows and offshoring. In the past two decades, many major U.S. companies have moved their operations to Mexico (under NAFTA) or to China, to take advantage of lower wages. The consequences of foreign investment in low-wage countries are roughly similar to the consequences of increased trade with those countries: raising the incomes of U.S. capitalists but lowering the incomes of some or most lower-skilled American workers.

Once again, both foreign investment and offshoring of jobs increase the U.S. economic pie by promoting greater efficiency in the economy. Once again, the increased income of the winners could, in principle, compensate the losers and thereby leave both American capitalists and American workers better off. And once again, the American political system has largely lost interest in income redistribution through taxes and transfers. The losers are told that it's just tough luck and they should fend for themselves.

It's important to understand that much of the firestorm over TPP and TTIP in fact has little to do with the gains and losses from trade or even from foreign investment and offshoring. Some of the biggest controversies are swirling around the regulatory framework that would be established by these trade agreements. Some of the proposed clauses in TPP would strengthen the intellectual property of the pharmaceutical industry, giving rise to legitimate concerns that the drug companies would have even greater monopoly power over their medicines, leaving even more people without access to lifesaving drugs. Many see the protections to workers on labor standards and human rights to be very weak and insufficient.

Yet perhaps the greatest controversy involves an arcane but very important part of the agreement: Investor-State Dispute Settlement, or ISDS. The ISDS provisions establish the right of foreign multinational companies to challenge the policies and regulations of host country governments and possibly to recover large financial damages. ISDS has given enormous, arbitrary, and unfair power to multinational companies.

Under ISDS, the foreign company's complaint is heard by an ad hoc, three-person tribunal that is not bound by the laws of the host country or even by precedents of ISDS tribunals. And there is no appeal. Moreover, only foreign companies can use ISDS. Domestic companies must go through the normal courts of law, and trade unions and other groups also have no protections under ISDS.

The original idea of ISDS was to prevent host governments from expropriating foreign investments. But now powerful companies are misusing ISDS to try to scare governments out of making and enforcing environmental, public health, or labor regulations. And if they fail to head off the regulations, they can use ISDS to win large financial damages from governments that are merely trying to defend the public good.

In one recent and egregious example, the Canadian company behind the notorious Keystone XL pipeline proposal, TransCanada, is now suing the U.S. government for $15 billion. The proposed pipeline would have carried Canada's high-carbon oil sands to U.S. refineries. Obama correctly canceled the project on the grounds of the pipeline's danger for global warming. Now TransCanada is suing the U.S. government for depriving the company of future profits on an investment that never took place! Such a complaint wouldn't have a prayer of prevailing in a normal U.S. court, under normal U.S. law (the government was just carrying out its proper function, after all). Yet TransCanada could win in an ISDS tribunal, where the rule of law does not apply.

The Obama administration argued that Congress should support the TPP in order to bolster America's credibility in Asia, claiming that TPP is key to U.S. national security. (China is not a signatory to the TPP; hence, claimed his administration, the TPP will give the United States an extra measure of power in Asia vis-à-vis China.) This argument is both naive and irresponsible. The real effect of TPP on national security is that it would increase the inequality of income and power in American society, weakening rather than strengthening national security.

Trade agreements should be voted up or down on the basis of their likely economic and distributional impacts, not on a fictitious argument about national security. TPP and TTIP, in their current form, deserve to be voted down. They should be reformulated to remove ISDS and should be combined with new tax and transfer measures to bolster the incomes of the working class. At that point, expanded trade should be supported. The economic pie would then be enlarged with the gains from trade shared broadly across the society. At that point, the public would be much more likely to support the passage of trade agreements that would offer widespread benefits to Americans and our trading partners.

8

DISPARITIES AND HIGH COSTS FUEL THE HEALTH CARE CRISIS

America's health crisis is really three crises rolled into one. The first is public health: America's average life expectancy is now several years below that of many other countries, and for some parts of the population, life expectancy is falling. The second is health inequality: The gaps in public health according to race and class are shockingly large. The third is health care cost: America's health care is by far the costliest in the world.

The Sustainable Development Goals put good health for all in a central place in sustainable development, notably in SDG 3. This goal calls for massive reductions of the burdens of both communicable and noncommunicable diseases. SDG 3 (Target 3.8) also emphasizes the need for universal and equitable access to quality health care, in order to "achieve universal health coverage, including financial risk protection, access to quality essential health-care services and access to safe, effective, quality and affordable essential medicines and vaccines for all."

Obamacare certainly did not solve these crises. Its main positive contribution has been to expand health coverage. Americans without health insurance fell from around 15.5 percent of the population in 2010 to around 9.1 percent today, a significant decline. Yet health care premiums are once again soaring, and the deeper causes of poor health are not being properly addressed. Obamacare amounted to a limited patch on a flawed system.

The numbers tell the story of the three crises. First, U.S. health outcomes are actually below the averages of other high-income countries in the Organization for Economic Cooperation and Development, or OECD.[1] U.S. life expectancy at birth in 2013 stood at 78.8 years, almost two years below the OECD average of 80.5 years. The United States also had higher than average infant mortality, a greater incidence of low birth weight babies, and a higher incidence of both breast cancer and prostate cancer.

Second, regarding the inequality of health care and health outcomes, the United States ranked thirty-third among the OECD countries in health insurance coverage as a share of the population, at 86.7 percent (rising to 90.9 in 2015 because of Obamacare), ahead only of crisis-stricken Greece.[2]

America's health outcomes are starkly unequal by class and race. According to the Health Inequality Project, the richest 1 percent of American men have a life expectancy at age forty of 87.3 years, a remarkable 14.6 years longer than the poorest 1 percent of American men, at 72.7 years. As for race, non-Hispanic white life expectancy in 2014 was 78.8 years, 3.6 years longer than for non-Hispanic blacks, at 75.2 years.[3]

Third, regarding the costs of the health care system, America's costs are out of sight, far above those of other countries. The United States spent a remarkable $8,713 per person on health care in 2013 (the most recent year of comparable OECD data), with the next most expensive country, Switzerland, spending just $6,325. As a share of national income, U.S. health spending came to a whopping 16.4 percent of GDP, compared with

11.1 percent for Switzerland. Since then, U.S. spending has increased to around 18 percent of GDP. The average health spending among all OECD countries was just $3,453, less than half of U.S. health care costs, and constituted an average 8.9 percent of GDP in the OECD countries as of 2013.

So the health crisis is stark enough. But what are its causes, and even more important, what are its solutions?

At the core of the crisis of health outcomes are the glaring economic, social, and political inequalities of the United States. The United States has the highest inequality of disposable income among high-income countries, and also the largest entrenched class of the poor and near-poor. All of America's social support systems—including health care, education, and the judicial system—are now clogged with human sorrows that would hardly exist in a more equal society: children who can't read, young people without requisite job skills, households in legal woes unable to afford lawyers, and poor people in ill health bearing the disease burdens of poverty.

Low-income Americans are in bad health for two main reasons. First, their social circumstances lead to more stress, mental illness, substance abuse, obesity, environmental harms, and other poverty-related disease burdens, which in turn entrench their poverty. Second, by dint of their poverty, they eat less healthy diets, have weaker links with the health care system (for example, no family doctor), cannot afford medications, disproportionately have lives disrupted by prison terms, and enjoy less leisure time.

The sky-high costs of medicines and health services exacerbate the problem at every turn. The most authoritative recent study of America's soaring health care costs is the 2012 report *Best Care at Lower Cost*, by the federal government's Institute of Medicine (now the National Academy of Medicine).[4]

That report found that the higher health care outlays in the United States—compared with Europe, Canada, Japan, and Australia—are due to the higher prices of health services (including drugs, hospital stays, outpatient visits, and medical procedures) rather than to a greater use or higher quality of those services.

For example, the cost of a bypass operation in 2013 averaged $75,345 in the United States compared with $36,509 in Switzerland, and a CT scan averaged $896 in the United States compared with $432 in Switzerland. Inpatient drug prices (measured in 2010) were also far lower abroad than in the United States—roughly half in the UK, Canada, and Australia.[5]

In other high-income countries, governments set the prices for health services in the course of negotiations with hospitals, doctors groups, and pharmaceutical companies. The government often covers the entire cost of health care out of tax revenues. Hospitals and doctors are often reimbursed a fixed sum each year for each insured individual (called "capitation") rather than reimbursed for each procedure ("fee for service"). Capitation encourages the health system to focus on prevention as well as treatment and to encourage health-promoting activities (like weight loss and exercise). Where other countries use fee for service, there is very often one price for a given service that applies for all providers and patients in a given region.

In the United States, the situation is different. America's hospitals, provider groups, and pharmaceutical companies set their prices in a bewildering array of negotiations between the providers and health insurers, governments (federal, state, and city), and individual patients paying out of pocket. Most providers are remunerated by fee for service rather than capitation.

The prices they charge vary widely by patient, even for the same procedures. There is no single price list. The providers charge what they can, depending on their market power. Some patients are covered by private health plans, and then prices are set between the providers and the health insurers. In other cases, the payer is government, so the negotiations are with public agencies. In still other cases, the patient is uninsured. Often the health providers charge the most to the uninsured who pay out of pocket.

The health providers have considerable market power, deriving from four sources: patents on medicines and devices; few provider groups in any given geographical market; the unilateral disarmament of Medicare in negotiations; and limits on the supply of health care workers, including doctors and nondoctors.

Consider drug prices and the role of patents. U.S. patent law grants an exclusive monopoly for twenty years, from date of filing, to the holder of a drug patent. This temporary monopoly enables the patent holder to raise retail prices far above production costs, ostensibly to give incentives for R&D. The problem is that the drug companies are using their monopoly pricing power to abusive extremes.

Gilead Sciences, for example, spent $11 billion in 2011 to purchase the patent for a wonder cure for hepatitis C from a small biotech company. Gilead paid the hefty sum of $11 billion knowing that it would turn around and charge the outrageous price of $1,000 per pill, even though the medicine costs around $1 per pill to manufacture. Gilead is earning more than $11 billion in profits every single year, recouping its purchase price countless times over. Many Americans with hepatitis C, including our veterans, are sick and even dying because they can't afford Gilead's extortionate prices.

A second source of monopoly power over prices is that, in many regions, there are now only one or two major health care providers. The problem of monopoly power is getting worse as mergers and consolidations reduce the number of major health providers in each region.

A third source of monopoly power is the fact that the 2003 federal law establishing Medicare Part D (covering prescription drugs) explicitly bars Medicare from negotiating with the drug companies. Gilead can set any price it wants without the Medicare program saying a word. This provision was stuck in the legislation, literally in the middle of the night, by the pharmaceutical industry's lobbyists and reflects the fact that the health industry is one of the biggest funders of congressional campaigns. In the 2016 election cycle, campaign contributions by individuals and companies in the health sector have totaled more than $200 million in support to candidates and PACs of both major parties.[6]

A fourth source of monopoly power results from various limits on the supply of health sector personnel. In 2013, the United States graduated just 7.3 medical students per 100,000 people, compared with an OECD average of 11.5 per 100,000 and a high of 19.7 per 100,000 in Denmark. The United States has only 2.6 doctors per 1,000 people, compared with an OECD average of 3.3 per 1,000. The United States could also augment the health workforce by allowing properly trained and supervised nondoctors to take on an expanded range of roles at lower cost, a process known as "task shifting."

Sky-high health care costs, combined with entrenched poverty and stagnant working-class incomes, are leading to devastating health outcomes. Recent research by Nobel laureate Angus Deaton and his coauthor, Ann Case, has shown that middle-aged working-class whites are now experiencing an unprecedented rise in mortality rates, not unlike the falling life expectancy that plagued middle-aged men in the Soviet Union in the years before its collapse. Rising death rates in the population signify a deep crisis in the social order, including the health system.

Obamacare increased health care coverage but did not solve the crisis of sky-high prices, and it may well have exacerbated it by adding government subsidies into a system marked by pervasive market power and lack of competition.

I therefore recommend the following policies to address America's urgent health care crisis.

First, as I suggest throughout this book, America should adopt policies to reduce income inequalities, end the overin-carceration of the poor, empower workers, clean and green the environment, and raise the social status of working-class families. Over time, such measures would help to reverse the epidemics of drug abuse, mental illness, obesity, and other diseases exacerbated by poverty and low social status.

Second, America should move toward universal health care coverage through public financing, as in Canada and Europe, with health providers (both private and not-for-profit) supplying coverage on the basis of capitation rather than fee for service. Capitation would encourage and enable health providers to offer supportive services (nutrition counseling, social support, health advising) that help to prevent, treat, and manage chronic conditions such as cardiovascular disease and adult-onset diabetes.

Third, the government should move to a system of price ceilings for medicines under patent through rational guidelines that balance the incentives for R&D with drug afford-ability and access. Economists have long argued that today's patent law does not do an adequate job of balancing the needed incentives for innovation with the assurance of access to affordable medicines. The situation became intolerable after the advent of Medicare Part D, with the government now spending vast sums for drugs and drug companies grossly abusing the system by setting outrageous markups on the cost of production.

According to campaign statements, the Trump administration is likely to move in the opposite direction: toward deregulation, cutbacks in public financing for the poor, and more attempts to make the "health market" work despite the illogic of trying to put public health into the category of a market commodity. It's not surprising that the stock market prices of healthcare companies soared in the first days after the November election. Yet doubling down on a market approach to health care is almost surely going to lead to even greater inequities and more price gouging. Sooner or later the United States will have to learn from the better performance of Canada, Japan, and Europe, where health care coverage, affordability, and outcomes are far better than those enjoyed by Americans.

9

A SMART ENERGY POLICY
FOR THE UNITED STATES

E nergy is the lifeblood of the economy. Without ample, safe, and low-cost energy it is impossible to secure the benefits of modern life, a point underscored by Sustainable Development Goal 7 to "ensure access to affordable, reliable, sustainable and modern energy for all." For two centuries, fossil fuels—coal, oil, and natural gas—offered the key to America's and the world's growing energy needs. Now, because of global warming, we have to shift and shift rapidly to a new low-carbon energy system.

Despite considerable hullabaloo, there is nothing very mysterious about the world's energy challenge. The Earth and moon are about the same distance from the sun, but the Earth is about 30 degrees Fahrenheit warmer than the moon because of the Earth's atmosphere, which traps energy from the sun and thereby warms the Earth. The heat-trapping effect of the atmosphere is called the greenhouse effect.

It's been known for about 150 years that atmospheric carbon dioxide (CO_2) is one of the "greenhouse gases" that contribute to the greenhouse effect. It's been known for 120 years that burning fossil fuels adds to the CO_2 in the atmosphere and thereby warms the planet. And it's been known with considerable precision for at least thirty years that atmospheric CO_2 is increasing rapidly and thereby causing global warming. The year 2015 was the warmest on instrument record (dating back to 1880), and 2016 was warmer than 2015.

For this reason, every nation in the world, including the United States, agreed in December 2015 in Paris to shift from a high-carbon energy system based on coal, oil, and gas to a low-carbon energy system based mainly on wind, solar power, hydroelectric power, nuclear energy, and geothermal power. The Paris Climate Agreement, which went into force in November 2016, is part of the sustainable development agenda as SDG 13. The Paris agreement aims to keep human-caused global warming to "well below 2 degrees Celsius" (3.6 degrees Fahrenheit) and to aim for no more than 1.5 degrees Celsius (2.7 degrees Fahrenheit), all measured relative to the Earth's temperature at the start of the fossil fuel era (around 1800). The warming of the Earth up to 2016 is already around 1.1 degrees Celsius, more than halfway to the globally agreed upper limit.

President Trump rejected climate science on the campaign trail and is surrounded by oil and gas interests. He seems intent, at the start of his administration, on turning the clock backward on climate policy, and has even threatened to pull the United States from the Paris Climate Agreement. This is certainly an issue where Americans will have to take a stand, to put the common good ahead of the narrow interests of the oil and gas lobby. The climate risks are so dire, the technological opportunities for energy transformation so positive, and the global urgency and consensus so clear, that any reversal of U.S. policy would necessarily be short-lived, though deeply frustrating and costly.

Moreover, climate policy and infrastructure policy are deeply intertwined. When we rebuild the transport, energy, communications, water, and other infrastructure, the key will be to build it sustainably, in a way that protects Americans and projects the U.S. economy into global competitiveness on leading zero-carbon energy and transport technologies. Otherwise we'll end up with a massively costly but useless infrastructure, and watch as other countries that make break-throughs in energy efficiency and zero-carbon technologies displace U.S. economic leadership.

The needed path forward is now relatively clear. Climate scientists have come up with a helpful tool called the "carbon budget" to guide us back to climate safety. Roughly speaking, the Earth's warming is proportional to the cumulative amount of carbon dioxide we burn and release into the atmosphere in other ways, such as by cutting down forests. To have a "likely" (that is, 67 percent) probability of staying below 2 degrees Celsius warming, humanity has a remaining carbon budget of around 900 billion tons of CO_2.

To put the remaining 900 billion tons into context, the world as a whole is currently emitting around 36 billion tons of CO_2 into the atmosphere each year. At the current rate of global energy use, the world therefore has only about 900/36 = 25 years of fossil use remaining if it is to stay below 2 degrees C, and even that stringent limit on fossil fuel use still leaves a 33 percent probability of exceeding 2 degrees Celsius! To add to the world's challenge, most of the poor countries desperately need to increase their overall energy use in order to benefit from energy-using modern technologies.

The name of the game is therefore a "transplant" of the world's energy system, replacing fossil fuels with low-cost, low-carbon alternatives, such as wind and solar power. Such a transplant may seem impossible, but it's actually well within reach. Most of the changes wouldn't even be noticed by most of us. Instead of driving a Chevy Malibu with a gasoline-burning internal combustion engine under the hood, we will instead drive a Chevy Volt with an electric motor under the hood. Instead of charging the Chevy Volt with electricity generated by a coal-burning power plant, the power plant would instead use wind, solar, nuclear, hydroelectric, or some other non-carbon energy source to generate the electricity.

Forward-looking engineers have already given us a pretty good road map from fossil fuels to zero-carbon energy. There are three guidelines.

The first is energy efficiency. We need to cut back on excessive energy use by investing in energy-saving technologies: LED lighting rather than incandescent bulbs, smart appliances that do not draw energy when not in use, better housing insulation and passive ventilation that cut heating needs (and heating bills), and so forth.

The second is low-carbon electricity. Depending on where you live, your power today is generated by a mix of coal, natural gas, nuclear power, hydroelectric power, and a bit of wind and solar power. By 2050, electricity should be generated by non-carbon sources (wind, solar, hydro, geothermal, nuclear, tidal, biofuels, and others) or by using fossil fuels together with technologies that capture CO_2 and pump it underground, a process called "carbon capture and storage" (CCS).

The third is called fuel switching. Instead of burning gasoline in the car, use electricity in its place; instead of burning heating oil to warm the house, use electric heating in its place; instead of using aviation fuel to fly planes, use advanced biofuels in its place; instead of a large industrial furnace, use a stationary hydrogen fuel cell (with the hydrogen produced by non-carbon electricity) in its place. For every current use of fossil fuel, we can find a low-carbon fuel substitute. Clever engineers have already shown how this can be done, but with practice and experience, we'll have even better options.

Most of us would hardly notice the difference in how our electricity is generated, our vehicles are powered, our homes are heated, or our steel is produced. The main thing we would notice is a slightly higher electricity bill and a vastly safer climate. Even the extra costs are likely to be transitory. As producers slide down the learning curve, the costs of electric vehicles, industrial fuel cells, fourth-generation nuclear power plants, and solar grids are likely to fall significantly.

We'll also enjoy the new low-carbon technologies more than today's. Smart electric vehicles not only will be cleaner and safer, but also will drive you to work while you read the morning news. The shift from coal to renewable energy and from gas-guzzlers to electric vehicles will also clear the deep smog from Delhi, Beijing, and other places that are now literally choking on their air.

Even if the Trump administration starts out as ideological and political champions of the old fossil-fuel industries, I think they won't get very far. The recognition of the climate dangers and energy-system needs is already a consensus beyond a narrow group of businesses and ideologues. Indeed, I'll bet that it will soon be a standard high school homework assignment across the country to chart America's future path from fossil fuels to zero-carbon energy. In each part of the country, students will be assigned a challenge: How can California, or North Dakota, or Boston make the least-cost and fastest transition?

California students will wax rhapsodic about the vast low-cost solar energy that can be tapped in the Mohave Desert. North Dakota students will sing the praises of North Dakota's remarkable wind power potential, big enough not only for the

Dakotas but also for the industrial Midwest from St. Louis to Chicago, Cleveland, and beyond. And Boston students will gaze northward to the vast lakes and rivers in Quebec stretching up to Hudson Bay, with enough hydroelectric power potential to provide the energy for the U.S. northeast, especially when combined with the vast onshore and offshore wind energy from Maine to Virginia.

The challenge is to make this transition quickly and seamlessly and without destabilizing the energy system or putting America's industrial companies at a competitive disadvantage with enterprises in China, Mexico, and India. The beauty of the Paris Climate Agreement is that all countries are now in this effort together. Not only American high school students but also students in Bangalore, India; Chengdu, China; and Monterrey, Mexico, will be completing the same homework assignment. And those students, in turn, will discover the vast hydroelectric potential of the Himalayas, the wind potential of Mongolia's Gobi Desert, and the solar energy in Mexico's Sonora Desert.

But is the transplant really worth it? Much of the transplant will pay for itself, in the sense of cleaner air, better appliances, and better services. Yet some parts of the energy transition will require extra costs for essentially the same energy services.

But here's a critical point to keep in mind. The last time Earth was just 1 degree Celsius warmer than it is now (a period called the Eemian, about 130,000 years ago), the ice sheets in Antarctica and Greenland had disintegrated to such an extent that the global ocean level was between 3 and 9 meters higher than today.[1] Today's small island economies would disappear.

I'm not talking only about the Maldives and Vanuatu. I live on a small island economy. It's called Manhattan. It would disappear too. Don't be smug, Boston. You too would be mostly under water.

But the risks transcend the inundation of New York City, Boston, Orlando, New Orleans, and countless other low-lying cities around the world. The global warming to date (with accompanying droughts and floods) has already destabilized food supplies in many parts of the world, and there is much worse ahead unless we undertake the energy transplant. Syria, to name just one case, experienced its worst drought in modern history between 2006 and 2010, leading to impoverishment, hunger, forced migration, and social instability that provided tinder for the war that broke out in 2011.

Yet Americans understandably fear the job displacements that would hit today's coal miners and oil roustabouts. Fortunately, the news on this front is entirely reassuring. At latest count, the total number of coal miners in America is 18,000, out of a labor force of 150,000,000. The total number of field workers in coal, oil, and gas is no more than 150,000, less than 0.1 percent of the workforce. We could very easily compensate or retrain the workers who will lose their jobs. Other workers in the fossil fuel sectors—accountants, managers, programmers, and the rest—will be needed in the new energy sectors and other parts of the economy.

There are really only a few true "losers" in America's energy transformation, and David and Charles Koch are perhaps among them. The Koch brothers own the largest private oil company in the world. In their narrow private interest, it might be better for them to defend their $100 billion oil industry investment and wreck the rest of the world. They, after all, can afford to buy new property above the rising sea level. Yet even on that narrow, callous calculus, it's probably not better for the Koch family children and grandchildren, who will suffer dire consequences from their parents' and grandparents' self-ish disregard for humanity's needs.

Recent excellent work by my colleague Dr. Jim Williams has charted the full scale of the U.S. energy transition to 2050.[2] (Again, using Williams's tools, students galore will soon be doing take-home problem sets.) It turns out that indeed renewable energy, nuclear power, and carbon capture and storage technologies offer a range of possible pathways to decarbonization. If you don't like nuclear power or CCS, it's still possible to make the transition to low-carbon energy, but at a higher cost. (Not surprisingly, the costs rise when options such as nuclear energy are taken off the table.)

The bottom line of Williams's scenarios is very reassuring. The cost of decarbonizing the U.S. energy system is around 1 percent or less of national income per year (currently around $180 billion per year out of today's $18.4 trillion US GDP). One percent of GDP is not cheap, but it is after all just 1 per-cent, a very small price to pay for global climate safety. Similar calculations, and similar bargains, will be the case for the energy transplant operation in other parts of the world. A few lucky places with magnificent wind, solar, or hydroelectric power will find the incremental costs of zero-carbon energy systems to be negligible.

If the energy challenge is all so clear, why isn't it happening? There are really three answers. First, some part of the energy transformation is already underway, with a rise in deploy-ments of wind and solar energy. Now that the climate risk is finally appreciated worldwide, the entire world is ramping up for energy transplant surgery. The second is that power-ful vested interests, including the Koch brothers, ExxonMobil until recently (but no longer), and Peabody Coal, told the American people lies about climate change for years and, even worse, funded the campaigns of politicians who have been willing to oppose climate legislation in return for campaign dollars.

And third, stunningly, because of the same lobbying pressures, there has been far too little long-term energy planning in Washington. The first job of President Trump and the new Congress should be to call upon the National Academy of Sciences and the great engineers across America to come up with an energy plan. Yes, this won't be the instinct or desire of the incoming administration, but I believe that the climate and energy reality will hit and hit hard, especially as infrastructure planning gets underway. It's the job of all Americans to speed the process of returning energy policy to science and sanity.

Washington had better make up for lost time. As the 2016 Nobel Laureate in Literature declared half a century ago, "Come Senators, Congressmen, Please heed the call, Don't stand in the doorways, Don't block up the halls . . . For the times they are a changin.'"

10

FROM GUNS TO BUTTER

The single most important issue in allocating national resources is war versus peace, or as macroeconomists put it, "guns versus butter." The vital role of peace for sustainable development is clear and unequivocal. As the world's nations put it in the new sustainable development framework: "We are determined to foster peaceful, just and inclusive societies which are free from fear and violence. There can be no sustainable development without peace and no peace without sustainable development."[1]

My argument is that the United States has been getting the war-and-peace challenge profoundly wrong, squandering vast sums and undermining national security as a result. In economic and geopolitical terms, America suffers from what Yale historian Paul Kennedy calls "imperial overreach." If the Trump Administration remains trapped in expensive Mideast wars, much less expands them, the budgetary costs alone could derail any hopes for solving our vast domestic problems.

On this score, we can have some glimmers of optimism. On the campaign trail, candidate Trump regularly criticized the United States for overstretch in the Middle East and called for improvements in relations with Russia. So far so good, and indeed such an approach is vital not only for peace but also for financing a bold domestic infrastructure program. Yet candidate Trump also rattled the saber vis-à-vis Iran and China. Feeding an anti-Iran frenzy would gravely worsen rather than stabilize the Middle East. A new U.S. arms race with China would remove any realistic chance of rebuilding the domestic U.S. economy. And worse, it could gravely imperil peace.

It may seem tendentious to call America an empire and speak of imperial overstretch, but the term fits certain realities of U.S. power and how it's used. An empire is a group of territories under a single power. Nineteenth-century Britain was obviously an empire when it ruled India, Egypt, and dozens of other colonies in Africa, Asia, and the Caribbean. The United States directly rules only a handful of conquered islands (Hawai'i, Puerto Rico, Guam, Samoa, the Northern Mariana Islands), but it stations troops and has used force to influence who governs in dozens of other sovereign countries. That grip on power beyond America's own shores is now weakening.

The scale of U.S. military operations is remarkable. The U.S. Department of Defense has (as of a 2014 inventory) 4,855 military facilities, of which 4,154 are in the United States; 114 are in overseas U.S. territories; and 587 are in forty-two foreign countries and foreign territories in all regions of the world.[2] Not counted in this list are the secret facilities of the U.S. intelligence agencies. The cost of running these military operations and the wars they support is extraordinary, around $900 billion per year, or 5 percent of U.S. national income, when one adds the budgets of the Pentagon, the intelligence agencies, homeland security, nuclear weapons programs in the Department of Energy, and veterans' benefits. The $900 billion in annual spending is roughly one-quarter of all federal government outlays.

The United States has a long history of using covert and overt means to overthrow governments deemed to be unfriendly to U.S. interests, following the classic imperial strategy of rule through locally imposed friendly regimes. In the case of Latin America between 1898 and 1994, for example, a remarkable study by historian John Coatsworth counts forty-one cases of "successful" U.S.-led regime change, for an average rate of one government overthrow by the United States every twenty-eight months for a century. And note: Coatsworth's count does not include the failed attempts, such as the Bay of Pigs invasion of Cuba.

According to Coatsworth's powerful study:

> Direct intervention involving the use of U.S. military forces, intelligence agents, or local citizens employed by U.S. government agencies occurred in 17 of the 41 cases. In another 24 cases, the U.S. government intervention was indirect. That is, local actors (usually military leaders) played the principal roles, but either would not have acted or would not have succeeded without encouragement or help from the U.S. government and its agents.[3]

This tradition of U.S.-led regime change has been part and parcel of U.S. foreign policy in other parts of the world—including Western Europe, Africa, the Middle East, and Southeast Asia—though historians have not yet followed Coatsworth's lead with such a detailed and precise accounting.

Wars of regime change are costly to the United States and often devastating to the countries involved. Two major studies have measured the costs of the Iraq and Afghanistan wars.

One, by my Columbia colleague Joseph Stiglitz and Harvard scholar Linda Bilmes, arrived at the cost of $3 trillion as of 2008.[4]

A more recent study by the Cost of War Project at Brown University puts the price tag at $4.7 trillion through 2016.[5] Over a fifteen-year period, this $4.7 trillion amounts to roughly $300 billion per year—more than the total outlays from 2000 to 2015 for the federal Departments of Education, Energy, Labor, Interior, and Transportation, the National Science Foundation, the National Institutes of Health, and the Environmental Protection Agency combined.

It is nearly a truism that U.S. wars of regime change have rarely served America's security needs. Even when the wars succeed in overthrowing a government, as in the case of the Taliban in Afghanistan, Saddam Hussein in Iraq, and Muammar Gadaffi in Libya, the result is rarely a stable government, and is more often a civil war. A "successful" regime change often lights a long fuse leading to a future explosion, such as the 1953 overthrow of Iran's democratically elected government and installation of the autocratic Shah of Iran, which was followed by the Iranian Revolution of 1979. In many other cases, such as the U.S. attempts (with Saudi Arabia and Turkey) to overthrow Syria's Bashar al-Assad, the result is a bloodbath and military standoff rather than an overthrow of the government.

What is the deep motivation for these profligate wars and for the far-flung military bases that support them?

During the period from 1950 to 1990, the superficial answer would have been the Cold War. Yet America's imperial behavior overseas predates the Cold War by half a century (back to the Spanish-American War in 1898) and has outlasted it by another quarter century. America's overseas imperial adventures began after the Civil War and the final conquests of the Native American nations. At that point, U.S. political and business leaders sought to join the European empires—especially Britain, France, Russia, and the newly emergent Germany—in overseas conquests. In short order, America grabbed the Philippines, Puerto Rico, Cuba, Panama, and Hawai'i, and joined the European imperial powers in knocking on the doors of China.

As of the 1890s, the United States was by far the world's largest economy, but until World War II, the United States took a back seat to the British Empire in global naval power, imperial reach, and geopolitical dominance. The British were the unrivaled masters of regime change, for example in carving up the corpse of the Ottoman Empire after World War I. But the exhaustion from two world wars and the Great Depression ended the British and French empires after World War II and thrust the United States and Russia into the forefront as the two main global empires. The Cold War had begun.

The economic underpinning of America's global reach was unprecedented. As of 1950, U.S. output constituted a remarkable 27 percent of global output, with the Soviet Union's roughly a third of that, around 10 percent. The Cold War fed two fundamental ideas that would shape American foreign policy up to the present. The first was that the United States was in a struggle for survival against the Soviet empire. The second was that every country, no matter how remote, was a battlefield in that global war. While the United States and the Soviet Union would avoid a direct confrontation, they flexed their muscles in dozens of hot wars around the world that served as proxies for the superpower competition.

Over the course of nearly a half-century, Cuba, Congo, Ghana, Indonesia, Vietnam, Laos, Cambodia, El Salvador,

Nicaragua, Iran, Namibia, Mozambique, Chile, Afghanistan, Lebanon, and even tiny Granada, among many others, were interpreted by U.S. strategists as battlegrounds with the Soviet empire. Often far more prosaic interests were involved. Private companies like United Fruit International and ITT convinced friends in high places (most famously the Dulles brothers) that land reforms or threatened expropriations of corporate assets were dire threats to U.S. interests, and therefore grounds for U.S.-led regime change. Oil interests in the Middle East were another repeated cause of war, as had been the case for the British Empire from the 1920s.

These wars destabilized and impoverished the countries involved rather than settling the politics in America's favor. The wars of regime change were, with few exceptions, a litany of foreign policy failures. They were also extraordinarily costly for the United States itself. The Vietnam War was of course the greatest of the debacles, so expensive, so bloody, and so controversial that the Vietnam War crowded out Lyndon Johnson's other, far more important war: the War on Poverty in the United States.

The end of the Cold War in 1991 with the demise of the Soviet Union should have been the occasion for a fundamental reorientation of U.S. guns-versus-butter policies. The end of the Cold War offered the United States and the world a "peace dividend," the opportunity to reorient the world and U.S. economy from war footing to sustainable development. Indeed, the Rio Earth Summit in 1992 established sustainable development as the centerpiece of global cooperation, or so it seemed.

Alas, the blinders and arrogance of American imperial thinking prevented the United States from settling down to a new era of peace. As the Cold War was ending, the United

States was beginning a new era of wars, this time in the Middle East. The United States would sweep away the Soviet-backed regimes in the Middle East and establish unrivaled U.S. political dominance. Or at least that was the plan.

The quarter century since 1991 has therefore been marked by a perpetual U.S. war in the Middle East, one that has destabilized the Middle East, massively diverted resources away from civilian needs towards the military, and helped to create massive budget deficits and the buildup of public debt. The imperial thinking has led to wars of regime change in Afghanistan, Iraq, Libya, Yemen, Somalia, and Syria across four presidencies: Bush Sr., Clinton, Bush Jr., and Obama. The same thinking has induced the United States to expand NATO to Russia's borders, despite the fact that NATO's supposed purpose was to defend against an adversary—the Soviet Union—that no longer exists. Mikhail Gorbachev has emphasized that NATO's eastward expansion "was certainly a violation of the spirit of those declarations and assurances that we were given in 1990" regarding the future of East-West security.

There is a major economic difference, however, between now and 1991, much less 1950. At the start of the Cold War in 1950, the United States produced around 27 percent of world output. As of 1991, when the Cheney-Wolfowitz dreams of U.S. dominance were taking shape, that figure was around 22 percent. By now, according to IMF estimates, the U.S. share is 16 percent, while China has surpassed the United States at 18 percent.[6] By 2021, according to IMF projections, the United States will produce 15 percent of global output compared with China's 20 percent. The United States is incurring massive public debt and cutting back on urgent public investments at home in order to sustain a dysfunctional, militarized, and costly foreign policy.

Thus comes a fundamental choice. The United States can vainly continue the neoconservative project of unipolar dominance even as the recent failures in the Middle East and America's declining economic preeminence guarantee the ultimate failure of this imperial vision. If, as some neoconservatives support, the United States now engages in an arms race with China, we rather than China are bound to come up short in a decade or two, if not sooner. The costly wars in the Middle East, if continued much less enlarged by the new administration, could easily end any realistic hopes for new federal investments in education, training, infrastructure, and the environment.

The far smarter approach will be to maintain America's defensive capabilities but end its imperial pretensions. This, in practice, means cutting back on the far-flung network of military bases, ending wars of regime change, avoiding a new arms race (especially in next-generation nuclear weapons), and engaging China, India, Russia, and other regional powers in stepped-up diplomacy through the United Nations and shared actions on the Sustainable Development Goals, including climate change, disease control, and global education.

Many American conservatives will sneer at the very thought that the U.S. room for maneuver should be limited in the slightest by the UN. But think how much better off the United States would be today had it heeded the UN Security Council's opposition to the wars in Iraq, Libya, and Syria. Many conservatives will point to Vladimir Putin's actions in Crimea as proof that diplomacy with Russia is useless, without recognizing that it was NATO's expansion to the Baltics and its invitation to Ukraine to join NATO that were primary triggers of Putin's response.

In the end, the Soviet Union bankrupted itself through costly foreign adventures such as the 1979 invasion of Afghanistan and its vast overinvestment in the military. Today the United States has similarly overinvested in the military and could follow a similar path to decline if it continues the wars in the Middle East and invites an arms race with China. It's time to abandon the reveries, burdens, and self-deceptions of empire and to invest in sustainable development at home and in partnership with the rest of the world.

11

INVESTING FOR INNOVATION

Of all of the purposes of government, one of the most important but often neglected is to mobilize science and technology to solve critical challenges. Modern society depends on highly complex technological systems for our safety and prosperity. Without these advanced technological systems, we'd have no chance to sustain national prosperity, much less to feed a global population of 7.5 billion people. Yet managing and improving those technologies requires a large and sustained investment by government alongside business and academia.

The key idea here is "directed technological change," meaning that scientists and engineers are pulled together to solve a complex challenge in the national interest. The argument is that the challenge is not only important and solvable but, because of its nature, is not the kind of challenge that the private sector alone will solve in a timely way on a for-profit basis.

Modern American history is replete with such endeavors. Indeed, one can say that they've helped to make the modern age. No doubt the most famous and consequential of all was the Manhattan Project during World War II. It is a stunning example of directed scientific and technological effort, showing how the most complex and cutting-edge scientific challenge can be met through targeted investments.

In 1938, on the eve of World War II, European physicists discovered the principle of nuclear fission (splitting an atom with a neutron, releasing enormous energy and more neutrons) and the possibility of a nuclear chain reaction. Within a year, far-sighted physicists realized that this could lead to a new kind of atomic bomb and the threat that Nazi Germany might get there first. Albert Einstein and Edward Szilard wrote a world-changing letter to President Franklin Roosevelt advising the president of this risk and urging a U.S. effort to develop such a weapon before Germany.

The Manhattan Project got underway intensively in 1942 and culminated in the atomic bomb in 1945. The project engaged many of the world's leading physicists in the effort and led to countless scientific and technological breakthroughs in a three-year period. Thus was born the nuclear era.

The mobilization of great minds, national laboratories, and private companies in pursuit of well-defined objectives is therefore not a quixotic quest. The lessons of the Manhattan Project were taken up after World War II in many important areas of national security, public health, new technologies, and general science. From the polio vaccine and the space age to the human genome and the Internet, directed technological change has repeatedly shaped and advanced the U.S. economy and the modern world.

These efforts have all been characterized by highly complex challenges; a sense of national urgency; and a mix of academic, philanthropic, commercial, and government organizations and financing.

Consider Jonas Salk's polio vaccine, developed more than half a century ago. In this case, the main financing came through a nonprofit organization (popularly known as the March of Dimes) launched by President Franklin Roosevelt in 1938. Jonas Salk led a scientific team at the University of Pittsburgh, from 1947 to 1954, to develop the vaccine. In 1955, the vaccine was tested and massively disseminated in an unprecedented public health campaign that engaged governments at all levels. Salk's vaccine, followed by Albert Sabin's vaccine a few years later, ended the U.S. epidemic. Polio is now on the verge of global eradication.

When asked who owns the patent on the polio vaccine, Salk famously replied, "There is no patent. Could you patent the sun?" As with the Manhattan Project, the Salk and Sabin efforts were not funded in search of commercial profits but rather in response to public need. The technology was to be deployed as a "public good" (national defense in the case of the atomic bomb, public health in the case of the polio vaccine), and commercial patents would have undermined the deployment of the technologies.

As with the Manhattan Project, the U.S. space program was launched as a national security effort, part of the Cold War competition with the Soviet Union. After the Soviet Union successfully launched its *Sputnik* satellite in 1957, the United States ramped up its own efforts. In May 1961, President John F. Kennedy inspired the nation with his call for America to commit itself to "achieving the goal, before this decade is out, of landing a man on the moon and returning him safely to Earth." The United States thereafter spent around 0.5 percent of GDP each year for the balance of the decade to support NASA's successful moon effort, mobilizing an estimated 500,000 workers and 20,000 companies. The spillovers in computing, semiconductors, aeronautics, telecommunications, materials sciences, and countless other areas of science and technology have of course been profound.

The Internet, as is widely known, was similarly given birth in a U.S. government effort again linked to national security. In this case, the Defense Department was interested in creating a network of computers that could support a resilient military command and control system supported by geographically dispersed access to a few major computer centers around the country. The core building blocks of the Internet, including data packet switching and the TCP/IP protocol, were developed as part of the Defense Department's ARPANET project that ran from the late 1960s until 1990. Building on ARPANET, the U.S. National Science Foundation during the 1980s established and developed a network linking major U.S. universities. From the 1990s onward, these publicly financed efforts became the foundation of the Internet and the vast commercial business world built upon it.

The list of such targeted technology efforts is long and inspiring. Moore's Law, the repeated doubling of computer power roughly every two years since the late 1950s, builds on industry and government technology road maps. The Human Genome Project, the successful mapping of the human genome, was a breakthrough program from 1990 to 2003 that engaged leaders in academic biology, private biotech startups, and major government research centers in the United States and abroad; the continuing spillovers in countless areas of public health, medicine, agronomy, archeology, anthropology, and many other disciplines remain vast. Even hydraulic fracturing ("fracking") to produce oil and gas from shale rock depended on the early initiatives of the U.S. Geological Survey (USGS).

For these reasons, the frequently heard political complaints about federal funding of early-stage technologies (such as the solar company Solyndra or electric vehicle Tesla) seriously miss the point of how our economy works and delivers cutting-edge technologies. Not every R&D project bears fruit, to be sure; such is, of course, the nature of cutting-edge research. Yet the track record of public-private-academic-philanthropic partnerships to advance science and technologies in critical areas is a key pillar of America's prosperity and technological excellence.

One of the threats to America's well-being, indeed, is the skimpiness of such efforts vis-à-vis areas of critical need. There are many highly promising and crucially important areas of R&D in which purely private and profit-driven efforts based on the incentives from patenting are falling far short of social needs.

Compare, for example, the $30 billion per year funding that is directed to biomedical science through the National Institutes of Health with the meager $7 billion per year that is currently spent by the federal government on research into renewable or other low-carbon energy technologies. The threat of climate change, we have seen, is on the scale of many trillions of dollars of damages per year, and the solutions depend on the rapid transition from fossil fuel–based energy to zero-carbon alternatives.

Consider two examples. First, the successful ramp-up of renewable energy depends on high-performance batteries that can store large amounts of energy per unit of weight; that can charge and discharge on repeated cycles; and that are safe and reliable, not catching fire in the phone or electric vehicle. Battery technology is a major scientific and technological challenge, with many promising leads but also the need for extensive research, much of it by sophisticated trial and error. Yet federal battery research investment is estimated to be around $300 million per year, a fraction of the need and the amount that could be readily absorbed by national laboratories and universities through federal research grants.

A second case is carbon capture and storage (CCS) technology, the only climate-safe way to deploy fossil fuels in the future. There are countless scientific and technological issues involved with CCS, including the feasibility of capturing CO_2 directly from the air; the lowest-cost ways to capture CO_2 from power plant exhaust gases; and the feasibility of geological storage of CO_2, depending on different kinds of geological formations and their risks of leakage. Some technologies are attracting private capital, but much of the science (such as the geological research) is almost entirely a public good that requires public rather than private financing. Yet worldwide, the scale of public financing for R&D related to CCS remains miniscule.

Other areas crying out for greater public investments in R&D include smart-grid systems to manage twenty-first-century infrastructure; fourth-generation nuclear energy; advanced materials sciences for environmental sustainability; global monitoring of earth systems using satellite imagery and remote sensing; supercomputing for climate and weather modeling; robotics and artificial intelligence (in countless aspects, including design, deployment, and ethics); the early identification and control of emerging epidemic diseases such as Zika and Ebola viruses; advanced agricultural technologies for crop resilience to climate change; improved nutrition; geriatric medicine (including the soaring costs of Alzheimer's disease); and cybersecurity and protocols for e-governance such as online voting, just to name some of the pressing and promising areas.

Because of America's chronic underfinancing of discretionary public spending, including the science-based agencies,

U.S. technological leadership is now at threat. Yes, America still has many of the world's leading universities and the greatest national depth of scientific and engineering capacity, yet the chronic underinvestment in science and technology (and in the public education at lower levels needed to foster future generations of scientists and engineers) puts the United States at severe risk.

Many might guess that the United States remains the world's most dynamic investor in R&D, but this is no longer the case. In R&D as a share of national output, the United States now ranks ninth among high-income OECD countries. U.S. R&D outlays are around 2.7 percent of national income, compared with more than 3.0 percent of GDP in Denmark, Finland, Germany, Japan, and Norway and more than 4.0 percent of GDP in Korea and Israel. In total dollars, China's outlay is currently around three-fourths of U.S. expenditure and is very likely to overtake it during the coming decade, unless of course the United States increases the share of GDP devoted to R&D.

As in past grand successes (develop an atomic bomb; find a polio vaccine; go to the moon; network computer systems; sequence the human genome), clear goals and long-term funding should undergird our future efforts. Projects should be guided by urgent public needs and by areas where public financing is vital because private financing is inappropriate or inadequate. That includes areas of basic science (where patents simply make no sense); challenges for which market-based approaches are inappropriate (such as control of epidemic diseases); goals that depend on the very rapid uptake of new technologies, so that private patents would clog rather than accelerate deployment (smart power grid protocols for integrating intermittent renewable energy); and goals that involve major social policies regarding risk and liability (nuclear energy and carbon capture and storage).

In many areas, such as disease control, crop productivity, and zero-carbon energy, much of the effort should be global, with costs and benefits shared across the world. Just as the moon shot turned into global cooperation in space, our global-scale challenges also behoove us to create international as well as national frameworks for expanded R&D. The Department of Energy under Secretary Ernie Moniz is currently engaging other countries to launch such an effort vis-à-vis low-carbon energy, dubbed the Mission Innovation Initiative.

Here is my recommendation for President Trump and the new Congress. Turn immediately to our glorious national institutions, the National Academies of Science, Engineering, and Medicine, for a report to the nation on the key areas for science and technology investments in the coming generation. Ask them to recommend an organizational strategy for a science-based scaling up of national and global R&D efforts. Call on America's research universities to add their own brainstorming to the work of the national academies. Later in 2017, the president and Congress should then meet in a joint session of Congress to set forth a new technology vision for the nation and an R&D strategy to achieve it.

12

TOWARD A NEW KIND OF POLITICS

If the dispiriting 2016 election proved anything, it proved that our political system is broken. Americans distrust the federal government and especially the Congress. These attitudes reflect underlying realities of American politics that need to change if other reforms in our society—health care, infrastructure, climate change, education, jobs, finance, and others—will have a chance. I propose several specific ways that America can get out of its political rut.

Over the ages, philosophers and scholars have viewed politics in highly divergent ways. Aristotle, the inventor of Western political theory more than 2,300 years ago, viewed politics as the way for a community to attain the highest public good. Laws, habits, and education should be designed to promote virtue among the citizenry, and virtuous citizens in turn should engage in political processes to promote happiness and well-being. Catholic social teachings have expressed a similar view of governance as the collective search for the common good.

Karl Marx and his followers, of course, take almost the opposite view. For Marx, politics is merely a "superstructure" that reinforces class relations. Government serves the interests

of rich capitalists even when the trappings of electoral democracies pretend to serve the interests of all citizens.

Democracy theorists like the scholar Robert Dahl view the
U.S. government (and similar representative democracies) as a
set of rules to ensure a wide representation and airing of ideas
and interests. Political elites compete for power through elections, but on the basis of representing disparate interests.

In a more cynical vein, "proceduralists" like Joseph
Schumpeter and Anthony Downs regard elections as processes
for the routine turnover of power, a way to throw out one
group of bums and replace them with another. One shouldn't
expect too much "common good" to arise from such a process,
argued Schumpeter, because in a world of divergent interests
and views, there is no common good after all.

Our predicament today is that Americans yearn for
Aristotle's vision but agree in diagnosis more with Marx
and a touch of Schumpeter. Americans want a problem-
solving government, one that lives up to the purposes of the
Constitution itself: "to form a more perfect union, establish
justice, ensure domestic tranquility, provide for the common
defense, promote the general welfare, and ensure the bless-
ings of liberty. . . ." Yet Americans feel that politics is failing
them, and for reasons similar to those argued 150 years ago
by Marx.

A recent detailed survey by the Pew Research Center
offers the evidence.[1] A majority of Americans want a major
role for the federal government, with more than 50 percent
of Americans seeing a major role for government in national
defense, the safety of food and medicines, immigration, the
economy, income security for retirees, access to health care,
and helping people get out of poverty. Yet there is great skepticism that government is doing its job. While 81 percent

of Americans believed the government should manage the immigration system, only 28 percent believed the government was doing a good job; 55 percent wanted the government to help people get out of poverty, but only 36 percent believed it was doing a good job on this challenge.

The overall trust in government—the belief that the federal government does "what is right" almost always or most of the time—has plummeted from around 75 percent of respondents in 1960 to around 20 percent today. Confidence in the government declined sharply in the 1960s and 1970s (with Vietnam, inflation, and Watergate), rallied a bit in the 1980s, fell in the late 1980s, rallied again in the mid-1990s, and then fell sharply after 2001, as shown in figure 12.1.

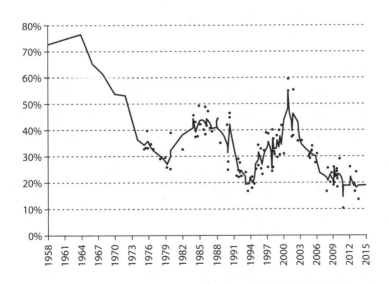

FIGURE 12.1 Public Trust in Government: 1958–2015

Source: Pew Research Center, "Beyond Distrust: How Americans View Their Government," November 23, 2015, http://www.people-press.org/2015/11/23/beyond-distrust-how-americans-view-their-government.

The causes of this sharp decline are well explained by other answers in the Pew survey. Essentially, the public does not feel represented by its elected officials. Enter Karl Marx. Of those surveyed, 77 percent said that elected officials "lose touch with people quickly"; 74 percent said that elected officials "don't care about people like me"; and 74 percent said that elected officials "put their own interests first." In addition, 67 percent replied that elected officials are "intelligent," but only 29 percent regarded them as "honest."

Americans view big money in politics as key to the problem. A remarkable 77 percent, with strong majorities in both parties, believe there should be limits on campaign spending; 76 percent believe that money has a greater influence on politics than in the past; and 64 percent believe that the high cost of campaigns discourages good candidates.

On this front, the broad public and the scholarly experts are converging. In a series of pithy studies and the important book *Affluence and Influence*, Martin Gilens and colleagues have shown that only the rich have influence on the political process.[2] In studying one policy issue after another, Gilens has shown that it is the population in the top income decile (10 percent), not the remaining 90 percent of the population, whose views prevail in the political process. In effect, the rich spend billions of dollars in lobbying and campaign contributions and thereby affect the allocations of hundreds of billions or even trillions of dollars in return.

We can be more specific on the sources of influence. While democracy theorists have viewed congressional politics as an arena for competing interests, the sad fact is that four very powerful corporate lobbies have repeatedly come out on top and turned our democracy into what might more accurately be called a corporatocracy.

Wall Street successfully engineered financial deregulation in the 1980s and 1990s and then the mega-bailouts that were needed thereafter. Serious financial fraud was repeatedly treated with kid gloves rather than criminal prosecutions. Today Wall Street still acts with impunity and with little regard for the long-term financing needs of the economy.

The military-industrial complex (MIC) has used its sway with Congress to ensure mega-defense budgets and a blind eye toward destabilizing arms sales abroad. The United States seems content to pump the Middle East and other regions to the brim with armaments, as long as they are American armaments. And the arms producers have cleverly designed their supply chains to ensure that major arms systems are produced in congressional districts throughout the country. As Eisenhower feared and warned us about the MIC, we have indeed created a war machine.

The health care sector, the third of the mega-lobbies, has successfully run up America's health costs to around 18 percent of GDP, compared with around 12 percent of GDP in Canada, Japan, and Europe. We noted earlier how the for-profit health care sector, including providers and pharmaceutical companies, exploit their market power to boost prices far above marginal costs. Americans pay with shorter lives and poorer health.

Big Oil has been the fourth of the great lobbies. With heavy campaign financing, intense lobbying, and massive outlays on public disinformation, Big Oil (and until recently Big Coal) has played the leading role in slowing America's response to global warming. It has been a spectacle to watch hundreds of members of Congress spout scientific nonsense, even relative to public opinion (which favors the large-scale deployment of renewable energy), all to curry a contribution from the oil industry.

Is there a way forward, when campaign financing and mega-lobbying have displaced the common good and have led Americans to despair about the functioning of the political system? Since incumbent politicians won't vote for campaign reform on their own, are we doomed to a vicious circle of big money, big corruption, failing public services, and a collapse of democratic rule?

Some think we are doomed; I do not. I believe, to the contrary, that we may well look back at the 2016 election as the moment when the corruption and sheer incompetence of Washington became so large and transparent that an era of reform finally got underway. Even if Washington goes badly in the wrong direction in 2017 and beyond, the American people may begin to mobilize for true and deep political reforms. Let me lay out the political reforms we need and how they might actually emerge from the current deep morass.

First, we need a political process that escapes the halls of Congress and engages the country in new ways. Think of how recent legislation such as Obamacare and the 2009 stimulus package were written: in the middle of the night in congressional backrooms with lobbyists holding the pen. The legislation was so complicated, in fact, that very few, if any, members of Congress knew what they were voting for. We discussed mysterious clauses buried deep in the text only years after passage.

The irony is that America is filled with problem solvers, from governors and mayors to local businesses, philanthropies, civic action groups, and academia. The depth of talent in America's colleges and universities is remarkable, and not just in the famed schools that top the annual rankings. This means that every state, and virtually every metropolitan area, has top-flight expertise that can be called upon for local problem solving, or to put the pieces of a national program together from the bottom up.

Second, we need a political process that transcends the dreary election cycle. Now that the 2016 election is over, attention will quickly shift to whether the Democrats can recapture the Senate in 2018 and who the Democrats will be running for the president in 2020. Yet what we really need is governance—most importantly, long-term plans to achieve long-term goals. The worst mistake of the new administration would be to announce some half-baked or completely misguided "plans" in the famous first 100 days, rather than to engage the entire nation in problem solving. Any so-called plans announced in the first hundred days would simply be the drafts of Washington lobbyists rather than real solutions to America's deep and complex ills.

By appealing for national engagement in problem solving beyond the halls of Congress, we would have the opportunity to chart a national course that isn't driven by the Washington electoral cycle, but rather by the cycles of raising children, rebuilding cities, and investing in new knowledge.

Third, we should return to our federal roots by fostering state and local solutions in addressing national goals. The federal government should adopt nationwide objectives, but encourage local and regional problem solving to meet them. Health care delivery, energy system transformation, and even future work patterns can and should evolve in distinctive ways in different parts of the country. The doctrine of "subsidiarity" should be applied: looking for solutions at the most local level of governance at which solutions can be found.

Of course the lobbyists will not roll over; those who financed the winning tickets in the 2016 campaigns will expect their due. The public needs to be ready to say a resounding

"No" to a Trump administration and Congress by lobby. In this regard, the prevailing gridlock on Capitol Hill may serve us well. To pass major legislation over filibusters and other blocking tactics, President Trump will have to win broad public support through national outreach, not just the support of political insiders and lobbyists.

Ultimately, our politics will be fixed when citizens rather than lobbyists are again in the political lead. And this will happen only when citizens are engaged in politics, not just at election time but also throughout the year, thereby pushing the lobbyists to one side. To restore an active and deliberative citizenry, we will need a new kind of political process, one that engages the citizenry on major issues, enabling citizens to help draft legislation, vote on issues of foreign policy, and weigh in on budget debates.

The political beauty of our online age is that it's now actually feasible—and urgently necessary—to reengage the public in just this way. In Aristotle's time, Athenian citizens assembled on the Pnyx hillside near the Acropolis to cast their ballots. For most of American history, elected representatives came together in the Congress to cast votes in the name of the people. Yet that kind of representation is now in name only, except if you happen to be a wealthy campaign contributor. In the coming age of e-governance, however, direct democracy will once again become feasible, and indeed inevitable. Like Athenians of old, we too will once again be in a position to cast our ballots and defend our honor. Democracy, I believe, will be restored, no matter the foot-dragging by today's political class.

13

RESTORING TRUST IN AMERICAN GOVERNANCE

More than any other threat facing America is the collapse of *civic virtue*, meaning the honesty and trust that enables the country to function as a decent, forward-looking, optimistic nation. The defining characteristic of the 2016 presidential election is that neither candidate was trusted. The defining characteristic of American society in our day is that Americans trust neither their political institutions nor each other. We need a conscious effort to reestablish trust, by making fair play an explicit part of the national agenda.

We have already noted the collapse in public confidence in the federal government. The collapse of trust in each other is equally striking. For decades, pollsters have asked Americans whether "most people can be trusted." And for decades, the proportion answering in the negative has been rising (figure 13.1).

There are probably two main reasons for this downward trend. The first is the sharp widening of income inequalities since the 1970s. The second is the widespread feeling that those at the top of the heap in income and power regularly abuse their wealth and influence. Donald Trump's relentless assertion in the 2016 campaign was that the system is "rigged,"

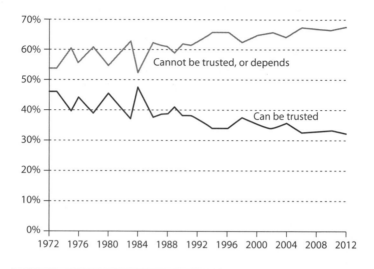

FIGURE 13.1 Americans on Whether "Most People Can Be Trusted,"
1972–2012

a claim that resonated widely despite the obvious irony that Trump himself has been a relentless rigger of the system.

The system is indeed rigged for the big corporate interests such as the drug companies that set drug prices a thousand times the production cost. It's rigged for the large IT companies such as Apple Inc. that deploy egregious tax loopholes that enable them to park their funds overseas in tax-free offshore accounts. It's rigged for the hedge fund managers who take home hundreds of millions of dollars in pay and then face a top income tax rate of 20 percent, far below what other, vastly poorer Americans must pay. It's rigged for the investment bankers that deliberately cheated their clients and then walked away with a mere slap on the wrist, if that. And the fact that the Clintons parlayed public office and a family foundation into a vehicle for vast personal enrichment was not lost on an unhappy and distrustful electorate.

Considerable social science research in recent years has given laboratory evidence to an ancient truth: that power and wealth indeed corrupt. Consider a fascinating psychology experiment published recently in *Nature*, a leading scientific journal.[1] The employees of a major international bank were divided randomly into two groups, a "control" group and a "treatment" group. Both groups were given forms to fill out at the start of the experiment. The control group was asked general questions. The treatment group was asked questions about their role in banking. Then each group was asked to flip coins and report honestly how many "heads" they flipped, being told that a greater number of heads would lead to a higher monetary award.

The control group reported that they flipped around 50 percent heads, an honest report. The treatment group claimed to have flipped around 58 percent heads, a dishonest report that exaggerated the proportion of heads flipped. The conclusion: Simply by being reminded that they were bankers (by filling out a form about banking), the treatment group was spurred to cheat. The psychologists concluded that the business culture of banking within that representative bank was a culture of cheating and greed.

One feels that America is like that today, especially at the top. This is an age of impunity, a time when the rich and powerful get away with their misdeeds, and are even lauded for them in some quarters. Donald Trump met the accusation that he had not paid income taxes for years with the response, "That makes me smart." Goldman Sachs CEO Lloyd Blankfein met the charge that his bank had cheated its customers with the response that they were "doing God's work." Hedge fund manager John Paulson was celebrated on Wall Street for his "cleverness" in conspiring with Goldman Sachs to bilk a German bank of hundreds of millions of dollars. The leaked emails showing how the Clintons mixed their public, private, and foundation activities simply confirmed for many unhappy Americans that this is how the system works.

The United States Supreme Court has shamelessly fed the impunity. In the infamous *Citizens United* case, the Supreme Court shockingly equated anonymous corporate contributions to political campaigns with free speech. The Court demonstrated that it had no realistic sense about how such corporate contributions have undermined the legitimacy of the political system. In a more recent case, the Supreme Court overturned the conviction of former Virginia governor Robert McDonnell, who had been convicted of fraud and extortion for taking gifts from a businessman promoting his health products to the state.[2] McDonnell walked away free from a shoddy and egregious abuse of office.

I have noted repeatedly that other high-income countries do not face these same trends. The U.S. pattern of rising inequality, falling trust, and increasing money in politics is not simply a reflection of the times or an inevitable side effect of democracy in the twenty-first century. Indeed, while many other countries are caught in a similar spiral of rising inequality, falling trust, and increasing corruption, many others are not. Canada, for example, has successfully avoided these extremes, even though we share a common North American economy and a 3,000-mile border. Decency and trust can be maintained even in our complicated, globalized times.

While there are no magic wands to restore social trust in the United States, there are important guideposts for citizens, businesses, and public officials. I suggest six key steps.

First, we should acknowledge the dangerous hold of the lobbyists and the super-rich on the political process. While many incumbents in office today will not sever their ties with their campaign contributors, citizens should sever their ties with politicians who rely on such contributions. Citizens' movements, social networks, and new political parties should establish a new norm for the coming elections: that they give political support (and small-scale donor support) only to candidates who reject large contributions from the rich and corporate interests. Campaign finance reform may arrive someday, but before that date it will be possible achieve progress by electing politicians not on the take.

Second, we should recognize that the rising power of the richest Americans has been key to the rising impunity in America today. Canada and the countries of Scandinavia have kept the lid on impunity by erecting legal, tax, financial, and cultural barriers to the accumulation of vast wealth and its insidious deployment in the political process. Yes, there are the very rich in all societies, but their outsized role in America's politics has been distinctive compared with the other high-income democracies.

Third, corporations are not people, despite the Supreme Court's confusion on this score. They are harder to shame, and are impervious to threats of imprisonment. For this reason, the rampant criminal activities of many powerful companies call for individual culpability of the CEOs and the corporate boards. When a major Wall Street bank pays billions of dollars in fines for egregious financial malfeasance, the CEO and board members should face personal accountability. This could include removal from office, banishment from the industry, and in justified cases, direct criminal indictment. Such individual accountability has been almost completely absent following the 2008 financial crisis. The CEOs who oversaw their companies' malfeasance were more likely to enjoy a state dinner at the White House than to face a day in court.

Fourth, the corporate doctrine of "shareholder responsibility" should be replaced, both legally and ethically, with a standard of "stakeholder responsibility." The difference is this: If a corporation today can get away with an action that boosts shareholder wealth by imposing harms on others, the prevailing corporate ethos is to take the action, especially if the action is deemed to be legal though damaging to the others. For example, in the name of shareholder profits, a drug company may boost the price of drugs to levels that cause great suffering; a company may pollute the air and water to avoid costs if the pollution is otherwise not illegal; a bank may aim for a quick and dirty profit by selling a toxic security to an unsuspecting buyer. In the stakeholder approach, such actions would be firmly rejected. The CEO and corporate board would aim only for policies that truly add value to society (true value added), not for policies that create shareholder value by imposing costs on others. Of course many companies already abide by such a standard, but many of the most powerful clearly do not, and even express their disdain for any restraints on their ability to maximize shareholder wealth.

Fifth, our former presidents and politicians need to exercise restraint in their money making. Barack Obama should break the recent pattern. Bill Clinton and Tony Blair decided to cash in after leaving office, creating the current atmosphere in which it seems that anything goes. Countless senators and congressmen have departed from Capitol Hill directly to K Street, from holding political office to lobbying their former colleagues. The practice is despicable and deserves the public's opprobrium. Of course, such behavior should also be blocked by a formal code of conduct and legislation. To achieve such reforms would require a strong and concerted public outcry.

Sixth, and most fundamentally, only by acting directly to reduce the inequality of wealth and income in the ways that I've outlined in earlier chapters—through fiscal redistribution, universal access to health and education, and environmental justice—can we restore the sense of a democratic system that is truly "of the people, by the people, and for the people."

The American people have still not heard a word of remorse from Wall Street CEOs for the 2008 crash; nor from the politicians for their egregious self-dealing and murky confusions of public office and private wealth; nor from the Supreme Court for handing America its most money-drenched politics in modern history; nor from the drug companies for jacking up drug prices to levels that are killing many Americans; nor from the hedge fund managers who have engineered tax breaks beyond egregious; nor from the CIA that has implicated Americans in endless failed wars and thereby endangered our lives with rising threats of terrorist blowback.

American disgust in the 2016 election was neither deplorable nor especially hard to understand. It was a rebuke to impunity. The anger will continue until the American system of governance, both public and private, is oriented around the common good rather than the private wealth and power of America's governing elite.

14

PROSPERITY IN SUSTAINABILITY

President John F. Kennedy inspired Americans to great undertakings by setting bold goals: to go the moon, to overcome racial discrimination, to make peace with the Soviet Union. "I believe that this nation should commit itself to achieving the goal, before this decade is out, of landing a man on the moon and returning him safely to the Earth," JFK told a joint session of Congress fifty-five years ago, and his words still stir us today. Similarly, he called on Americans to sign a Partial Nuclear Test Ban Treaty with the Soviet Union, declaring that "our attitude [toward peace] is as essential as theirs."

Our generation's needs are different, but the spirit of setting great goals and devoting the resources to achieve them can move America and the world once again.

Our generation's greatest challenge is sustainable development, meaning a nation that is prosperous, fair, and environmentally sustainable. Our nation's goals should be the Sustainable Development Goals for the year 2030. The U.S. government signed those goals along with the other 192 United Nations member states on September 25, 2015, but our government has so far neglected them. The United States should enthusiastically embrace the SDGs as if our future depends on them. It does.

It may seem unlikely to most that President Trump will take up the SDGs, and indeed he may not. But Americans across the country should do so. They are our best compass back to a decent society, one that is united for the common good. We should urge President Trump and the Congress to take on sustainable development, and hope they do so. But if they don't, it is our job as citizens to step forward to meet our generation's responsibilities. In cities, campuses, communities, and businesses throughout the country, the SDGs can become the guideposts and rallying cry for a generation looking to heal wounds, avert climate disaster, and promote the common good.

Sustainable development is more than a checklist of policies. It is a coherent idea that holds firmly that economic growth can and should be fair, inclusive, and environmentally sustainable. It calls for a society very different from the one we have today, where the elites run the show and the rest are compelled to scramble to make do the best they can.

The Sustainable Development Goals were negotiated by the world's governments over a three-year period, starting in 2012, and were adopted unanimously in 2015. That already tells us something, given that the world's nations usually agree on very little. They agreed on the SDGs out of the conviction that all parts of the world share the same grim reality of massive environmental threats and that most are also reeling from rising inequality and political instability brought on by rapid technological changes, globalization, pervasive tax evasion, widespread corruption, and unethical activities by many multinational corporations. These countries also adopted the Paris Climate Agreement, out of the same sense of shared fate if the world fails to act to stop global warming.

Yet more than fear spurred both the SDGs and the Paris agreements. These global agreements were also underpinned by hope, specifically by the sense that the current technological revolution offers a way forward that can end extreme poverty, promote economic development, and protect the environment at the same time.

The Sustainable Development Goals follow a second precept of JFK: that goal setting, and the practical work toward those goals, can be an inspiration and motivation to the public. As he was pursuing the Nuclear Test Ban Treaty in 1963, Kennedy laid out a sequence of steps that included the treaty and other supportive measures. Kennedy explained the logic of his approach this way: "By defining our goal [for peace] more clearly, by making it seem more manageable and less remote, we help all people to see it, to draw hope from it, and to move irresistibly toward it."

Kennedy also never shied away from the hard truths about his initiatives. Of the moon project, he noted that "none will be so difficult or expensive to accomplish." Of the nuclear treaty, he noted that "This treaty is not the millennium. It will not resolve all conflicts . . . but it is an important first step—a step toward peace—a step toward reason—a step away from war."

For many years, the United States has not set clear and compelling goals for fixing the economy, ending climate change, or addressing inequality. Of course, President Obama has launched various initiatives, but these have been incremental and, typically, without clear end points in mind. Many of us feel deflated by the dispiriting 2016 election campaign and the widespread belief that America's greatest days are behind it. America needs and can achieve great goals in the years ahead.

What, then, do the seventeen Sustainable Development Goals mean for the United States? They are a unique opportunity to embrace the deep change our nation desperately needs. They are an opportunity to point to the mountain summit and decide how we are going to get there. As Kennedy said of the moon shot, "We choose to go to the moon in this decade and do the other things, not because they are easy but because they are hard, because that goal will serve to organize and measure the best of our energies and skills."

Early in 2017, with a new president and Congress, our nation should collectively adopt American Sustainable Development Goals for 2030. In table 14.1, I list seventeen specific bold goals that we might embrace and briefly describe several of them:

- The United States has the highest poverty rate of any advanced economy, standing at 17 percent, according to the International Organization for Economic Cooperation and Development definition of the poverty line (household income at less than half of the median income). By contrast, Denmark has the lowest, at 6 percent. In line with SDG 1, America should pledge measures to reduce the poverty rate to 8.5 percent or below by 2030, cutting the poverty rate by at least half.
- The United States has the highest obesity rate of any advanced economy, standing at 36 percent, compared with the lowest rate, in Japan, of just 3 percent. In line with SDG 2, America should pledge public health actions to aim to reduce the obesity rate to below 10 percent by 2030.
- Life expectancy in United States lags behind that of the world's leading nations by at least four years, 79.3 in the United States compared with 83.7 in Japan. In line with

TABLE 14.1 Sustainable Development Goals for America in 2030

SDG	Target	Actual 2015	Target 2030
SDG 1 End Poverty	Poverty rate	17%	8%
SDG 2 Nutrition	Obesity rate	34%	10%
SDG 3 Health	Life expectancy	78 years	85 years
SDG 4 Education	Student debt	$1 trillion	$200 billion
SDG 5 Gender Equality	Women in Congress	19.40%	50%
SDG 6 Water	Water stress (WRI)	2.9/5.0	1.0/5.0
SDG 7 Modern Energy Services	Renewable energy as share of total	6.30%	30%
SDG 8 Decent Work	Youth without work or training	15%	5%
SDG 9 Industry and Innovation	R&D as share of GDP	2.80%	4%
SDG 10 Inequality	Gini coefficient	.41	.30
SDG 11 Sustainable Cities	Wastewater treated	63.70%	100%
SDG 12 Sustainable Consumption	Non-recycled waste per person	1.7 tons	<1 ton
SDG 13 Climate Change	CO_2 emissions per person	17 tons	<8 tons
SDG 14 Ocean Health	Protected marine sites	18.20%	50%
SDG 15 Terrestrial Health Protected	Terrestrial sites protected as share of total area	10.60%	25%
SDG 16 Peaceful Society	Prison population	716/100,000	100/100,000
SDG 17 Global Partnership	Development aid (% GDP)	0.17%	0.70%

SDG 3, the United States should pledge that life expectancy will reach at least 85 years by 2030 (compared with a
projected 86 years in Japan).

- The United States has student debt of $1.2 trillion because
  of a flawed system of financing of higher education. Many

other countries, with comparable university enrollment rates, have no student debt. In line with SDG 4, America should pledge to cut student debt to below $200 billion by 2030 while raising college completion rates from 33 percent to at least 50 percent of 25- to -29-year-olds.

- As the most unequal of all of the high-income OECD countries, the United States should pledge to undertake a range of policies, including taxes and transfers, health care, education, and corporate reforms, to narrow income inequalities decisively. In line with SDG 10, the United States would aim for a decline in the Gini coefficient on disposable income from the current rate of 0.41 to 0.30 or below as of 2030.

- The United States is one the highest emitters of dangerous greenhouse gases, with annual CO_2 emissions per American at sixteen tons, roughly three times the world average. By shifting rapidly to low-carbon energy, in line with SDGs 7 and 13, the United States should pledge to cut 2030 per capita emissions to below eight tons, based on a long-term pathway for reaching net zero emissions in the second half of the century, as called for in the Paris climate agreement.

- The United States has the highest rate of imprisonment of any advanced economy, with 716 inmates per 100,000 people, compared with a range of just 65 to 75 per 100,000 in the Scandinavian countries. America has cruelly locked up a generation of young African Americans, turning petty crimes (and sometimes no crimes at all) into wrecked lives for a generation. The United States should urgently reform its penal code to cut the prison population decisively and help young minority men gain skills and jobs for productive lives. In line with SDG 16, America should aim to reduce the prison population to no more than 100 per 100,000 by 2030, while continuing to reduce the rate of violent crime.

- Among the high-income countries, the U.S. government offers the lowest share of development assistance to the world's poor nations, just 0.17 percent of GDP compared with the global target of 0.70 percent of GDP. Our foreign policy is overmilitarized, thereby undermining our long-term national security. In line with SDG 17, the United States should increase its development aid to the global target by 2030 by shifting about 10 percent of current military-related outlays. The increased aid should be targeted at education, health, and infrastructure in today's poor and unstable countries.

The point is that the United States urgently needs to achieve such targets to remain among the world's better performers. None of the goals outlined is utopian or out of reach. Indeed, in every case, there would still be countries outperforming the United States on each particular dimension of sustainable development.

This kind of bold goal-setting is familiar from America's own past, which once inspired the world. Yet in American politics today, we feel out of shape, a kind of policy "ill health" not unlike our widespread physical ill health. The United States lacks the kind of strategic agencies and planning ministries that in other high-income countries help to set national goals and chart pathways to success. In Sweden, for example, the coordinating responsibilities for the SDGs have been placed within the Ministry of Public Administration, which works with the Riksdag (parliament) and local governments to implement the nationwide SDG strategy.

To achieve the SDG targets for 2030, we need, most of all, long-term thinking and strategic plans of action that show how key stakeholders—including governments at all levels, civil society, academia, and business—can contribute to the goals. By "defining our goal more clearly," in JFK's terms, we can mobilize the long-term public support to put them into operation. But we must recognize that, with more than two decades of little public planning, we are rusty, to say the least. Here, then, are three tips for the new administration:

First, the United States has more world-class expertise in its universities, businesses, think tanks, and foundations than just about any other country in the world. Call on them to contribute. Roadmaps to 2030 and beyond cannot be set by the White House, Congress, or lobbyists, and not in some artificial "first 100 days" of the next administration. Long-term strategies should be the result of a nationwide deliberation that engages top thinkers and doers throughout the country.

Second, the president has at the administration's disposal the National Academies of Sciences, Engineering, and Medicine, just down the block from the White House. These three world-leading institutions should be tasked with mobilizing the nation's best minds to find practical pathways to the 2030 goals. They, together with the great foundations in this country—Gates, Carnegie, Ford, Rockefeller, MacArthur, and others—can in turn tap the innovators, engineers, entrepreneurs, and social activists to mobilize for the 2030 SDGs.

Third, to an extent unmatched anywhere else in the world, the United States has a depth of knowledge, competence, and eagerness to contribute among its roughly 4,000 colleges and universities. Every congressional district has one or more high-quality science departments to explain to the member of Congress that climate change is real, serious, and solvable.

Every district has a university faculty that can help to identify local solutions to promote the 2030 goals.

In short, in a country with the wealth of knowledge, technology, and skills of the United States, we don't need to settle for a rank of twenty-second out of thirty-four OECD countries in sustainable development. By setting ambitious Sustainable Development Goals, and by engaging thought leaders across the country, the United States could once again set the standard for policy boldness and innovation and inspire other nations, even today's adversaries, to work together for a better world.

SUGGESTED FURTHER READINGS

The following materials will be helpful to readers seeking a deeper exploration of the topics in this book.

Mazzucato, Mariana. *The Entrepreneurial State*. New York: Anthem, 2013.

This book demonstrates the crucial role of the public sector in directed technological change. A creative, important, and influential study.

Sachs, Jeffrey. *The Age of Sustainable Development*. New York: Columbia University Press, 2015.

I explore the detailed agenda for economic development, social inclusion, and environmental sustainability embodied in the 17 SDGs.

Sachs, Jeffrey. *The Price of Civilization*. New York: Random House, 2012.

In this previous book on the U.S. political economy, I explore at somewhat greater length several of the themes described here: the low level of taxation, the excessive role of major corporate lobbies, and the need for political reforms.

Sachs, Jeffrey. *To Move the World: JFK's Quest for Peace*. New York: Random House, 2013.

In 1963, President John F. Kennedy "moved the world" by pursuing a bold strategy of peace with the Soviet Union at the height of the Cold War. This is a historic demonstration of national leadership through bold and creative goal setting.

United Nations. *Transforming Our World: The 2030 Agenda for Sustainable Development*. A/RES/70/1.

All 193 countries of the UN have adopted the 2030 Agenda. The text is therefore a core document for global cooperation in the coming years.

UN Framework Convention on Climate Change (2015). The Paris Agreement.

The Paris Agreement is the most important global agreement to control human-induced climate change since the signing of the UN Framework Convention on Climate Change in 1992. Unanimously adopted and put into force in November 2016, the Paris Climate Agreement will be at the very center of global diplomacy for years if not decades ahead.

UN Sustainable Development Solutions Network (SDSN), *The Deep Decarbonization Pathways Project*, 2015.

This project of the SDSN helped to create a framework for long-term planning of the transition to a low-carbon economy.

UN Sustainable Development Solutions Network (2016). *The SDG Index and Dashboards*.

The SDSN will issue an annual report on each country's progress towards the SDGs. The 2016 report is the initial issue.

NOTES

PREFACE

1. Risky Business Project, "Risky Business: A Climate Risk Assessment for the United States," June 2014, https://riskybusiness .org/site/assets/uploads/2015/09/RiskyBusiness_Report _WEB_09_08_14.pdf; U.S. Global Change Research Program, "National Climate Assessment," 2014, http://nca2014 .globalchange.gov/.

1. WHY WE NEED TO BUILD A NEW AMERICAN ECONOMY

1. McKinsey Global Institute, "Poorer Than Their Parents? Flat or Falling Incomes in Advanced Economies," July 2016, http://www.mckinsey.com/global-themes/employment -and-growth/poorer-than-their-parents-a-new-perspective-on -income-inequality.
2. Emmanuel Saez, "Striking It Richer: The Evolution of Top Incomes in the United States (updated with 2015 preliminary estimates)," Working Paper, University of California at Berkeley, June 30, 2016.
3. Daron Acemoglu, David Autor, David Dorn, Gordon H. Hanson, and Brendan Price, "Import Competition and the Great US Employment Sag of the 2000s," *Journal of Labor Economics* 34, no. S1 (Part 2, January 2016): S141–S198.

4. For a recent example, see Deloitte, "Technology and People: The Great Job-Creating Machine," August 2015, https://www2.deloitte.com/content/dam/Deloitte/uk/Documents/finance/deloitte-uk-technology-and-people.pdf.

5. Congressional Budget Office, "The 2016 Long-Term Budget Outlook," July 2016, www.cbo.gov/publication/51580.

6. Gordon, Robert. *The Rise and Fall of American Growth* (Princeton, N.J.: Princeton University Press, 2016).

7. United Nations, *Transforming Our World: The 2030 Agenda for Sustainable Development*, 2015, https://sustainabledevelopment.un.org/post2015/transformingourworld. Note that subsequent mentions of the SDGs in this book refer to this source.

8. United Nations Framework Convention on Climate Change, *The Paris Agreement*, 2015, http://unfccc.int/paris_agreement/items/9485.php.

9. Bertelsmann Stiftung and UN Sustainable Development Solutions Network (SDSN), *The SDG Index and Dashboard*, 2016, http://sdgindex.org.

3. DECODING THE FEDERAL BUDGET

1. Auxier, Richard, Len Burman, Jim Nunns, and Jeff Rohaly, *An Analysis of Hillary Clinton's Tax Proposals*, Tax Policy Center, March 3, 2016, http://www.taxpolicycenter.org/publications/analysis-hillary-clintons-tax-proposals/full.

2. The Office of Management and Budget produces ten-year scenarios that show the projected decline in nondefense discretionary. For the most recent, see Table S-6, p. 28 of the Mid-Session Review Fiscal Year 2017, Office of Management and Budget, July 2016, https://www.whitehouse.gov/sites/default/files/omb/budget/fy2017/assets/17msr.pdf.

3. Congressional Budget Office, *The 2016 Long-Term Budget Outlook*, July 2016, www.cbo.gov/publication/51580.

4. John Helliwell, Richard Layard, and Jeffrey Sachs, eds., *World Happiness Report 2016*, http://worldhappiness.report/wp-content/uploads/sites/2/2016/03/HR-V1_web.pdf.

4. SUSTAINABLE INFRASTRUCTURE AFTER THE AUTOMOBILE AGE

1. American Society of Civil Engineers, *Failure to Act: Closing the Infrastructure Investment Gap for America's Economic Future* (Boston: Economic Development Research Group, 2016).

2. The Deep Decarbonization Pathways Project (DDPP) is a global collaboration of energy research teams charting practical pathways to deeply reducing greenhouse gas emissions in their own countries. It is predicated on taking seriously what is needed to limit global warming to 2°C or less. See J. H. Williams, B. Haley, F. Kahrl, J. Moore, A. D. Jones, M. S. Torn, and H. McJeon, *Pathways to Deep Decarbonization in the United States*, The U.S. Report of the Deep Decarbonization Pathways Project of the Sustainable Development Solutions Network and the Institute for Sustainable Development and International Relations, 2014. Revision with technical supplement, November 16, 2015.

5. FACING UP TO INCOME INEQUALITY

1. Bernadette D. Proctor, Jessica L. Semega, and Melissa A. Kollar, "Income and Poverty in the United States: 2015," U.S. Census Bureau Report Number P60-256, September 13, 2016, http://www.census.gov/library/publications/2016/demo/p60-256.html.

2. Emmanuel Saez, "Striking It Richer: The Evolution of Top Incomes in the United States (updated with 2015 preliminary estimates)," Working Paper, University of California at Berkeley, June 30, 2016.

3. Jeffrey D. Sachs and Howard J. Shatz, "Trade and Jobs in U.S. Manufacturing," *Brookings Papers on Economic Activity* 1994, no. 1 (1994): 1–84.

6. SMART MACHINES AND THE FUTURE OF JOBS

1. OECD Better Life Index, "Education," http://www.oecdbetterlifeindex.org/topics/education/, showing an expected 17.1 years of education in the United States between the ages of 5 and 39.

2. American Time Use Survey 2015, http://www.bls.gov/news .release/pdf/atus.pdf. See Table 1, showing average work of 3.19 hours, or 3 hours, 11 minutes.

3. Claudia Goldin and Lawrence F. Katz, *The Race Between Education and Technology* (Cambridge, Mass.: Harvard University Press, 2010).

4. Carl Benedikt Frey and Michael A. Osborne, *The Future of Employment: How Susceptible Are Jobs to Computerisation?* September 17, 2013, http://www.oxfordmartin.ox.ac.uk /downloads/academic/The_Future_of_Employment.pdf; Michael Chui, James Manyika, and Mehdi Miremadi, "Where Machines Could Replace Humans—and Where They Can't (Yet)," *McKinsey Quarterly*, July 2016, http://www.mckinsey .com/business-functions/digital-mckinsey/our-insights/where -machines-could-replace-humans-and-where-they-cant-yet.

5. *Economic Report of the President: Together with the Annual Report of the Council of Economic Advisers*, February 2016, https://www.whitehouse.gov/sites/default/files/docs /ERP_2016_Book_Complete%20JA.pdf.

8. DISPARITIES AND HIGH COSTS FUEL THE HEALTH CARE CRISIS

1. Organisation for Economic Cooperation and Development, *Health at a Glance 2015: OECD Indicators*, http://dx.doi .org/10.1787/health_glance-2015-en.

2. Jessica C. Barnett and Marina S. Vornovitsky, "Health Insurance Coverage in the United States: 2015," U.S. Census Bureau Report Number P60-257, September 13, 2016, http:// www.census.gov/library/publications/2016/demo/p60-257 .html.

3. Raj Chetty, Michael Stepner, Sarah Abraham, Shelby Lin, Benjamin Scuderi, Nicholas Turner, Augustin Bergeron, and David Cutler, "The Association Between Income and Life Expectancy in the United States, 2001–2014," *JAMA* 315, no. 16 (April 26, 2016):1750–1766; see also https://healthinequality .org.

4. Institute of Medicine, *Best Care at Lower Cost: The Path to Continuously Learning Health Care in America* (Washington, D.C.: The National Academies Press, 2013).

5. International Federation of Health Plans, *2013 Comparative Price Report: Variation in Medical and Hospital Prices by Country*, https://static1.squarespace.com/static/518a3cfee4b0a77d03a62c98/t/534fc9ebe4b05a88e5fbab70/1397737963288/2013+iFHP+FINAL+4+14+14.pdf.

6. Center for Responsive Politics, "Totals by Sector: Election Cycle 2016," https://www.opensecrets.org/overview/sectors.php.

9. A SMART ENERGY POLICY FOR THE UNITED STATES

1. James Hansen et al., "Ice Melt, Sea Level Rise and Superstorms: Evidence from Paleoclimate Data, Climate Modeling, and Modern Observations That 2C Global Warming Could Be Dangerous," *Atmospheric Chemistry and Physics* 16 (2016): 3761–3812.

2. James H. Williams et al., *Pathways to Deep Decarbonization in the United States*, U.S. Report of the Deep Decarbonization Pathways Project of the Sustainable Development Solutions Network and the Institute for Sustainable Development and International Relations, November 2014; Revision with Technical Supplement, November 16, 2015.

10. FROM GUNS TO BUTTER

1. United Nations, *Transforming Our World: The 2030 Agenda for Sustainable Development*, 2015, https://sustainabledevelopment.un.org/post2015/transformingourworld.

2. Department of Defense, *Base Structure Report – Fiscal Year 2015 Baseline*, http://www.acq.osd.mil/eie/Downloads/BSI/Base%20Structure%20Report%20FY15.pdf.

3. John Coatsworth, "Liberalism and Big Sticks: the Politics of U.S. Interventions in Latin America, 1898–2004, 2006, at http://academiccommons.columbia.edu/catalog/ac:204082.

4. Joseph Stiglitz and Linda Bilmes, *The Three Trillion Dollar War: The True Cost of the Iraq Conflict* (Melbourne: Allen Lane / Penguin, 2008).
5. Neta Crawford, "US Budgetary Costs of Wars through 2016: $4.79 Trillion and Counting: Summary of Costs of the US Wars in Iraq, Syria, Afghanistan and Pakistan and Homeland Security," Brown University, Watson Institute of International & Public Affairs, September 2016.
6. See the IMF World Economic Outlook Database October 2016, at http://www.imf.org/external/pubs/ft/weo/2016/02 /weodata/index.aspx.

12. TOWARD A NEW KIND OF POLITICS

1. Pew Research Center, "Beyond Distrust: How Americans View Their Government," November 23, 2015, http://www .people-press.org/2015/11/23/beyond-distrust-how-americans -view-their-government.
2. Martin Gilens, *Affluence and Influence* (Princeton, N.J.: Princeton University Press, 2013).

13. RESTORING TRUST IN AMERICAN GOVERNANCE

1. Alain Cohn, Ernst Fehr, and André Maréchal, "Business Culture and Dishonesty in the Banking Industry," *Nature* 516 (December 4, 2014): 86–89.
2. *McDonnell v. United States*, October Term 2015, https://www .supremecourt.gov/opinions/15pdf/15-474_ljgm.pdf.